Using Deliberative Techniques in the English as a Foreign Language Classroom

A Manual for Teachers of Advanced Level Students

ෆ৪৯

Nancy Claxton, Ed.D.

Using Deliberative Techniques in the English as a Foreign Language Classroom

A Manual for Teachers of Advanced Level Students

☙❧

Nancy Claxton, Ed.D.

INTERNATIONAL DEBATE EDUCATION ASSOCIATION

NEW YORK * AMSTERDAM * BRUSSELS

Published by

international debate education association

400 West 59th Street / New York, NY 10019

Copyright © 2008 by International Debate Education Association

Library of Congress Cataloging-in-Publication Data

Claxton, Nancy.
  Using deliberative techniques in the English as a foreign language classroom: a manual for teachers of advanced level students / Nancy Claxton.
     p. cm.
  ISBN 978-1-932716-29-0
  1. English language--Study and teaching--Foreign speakers--Handbooks, manuals, etc. I. Title.
  PE1128.A2C535 2007
  428.0071--dc22

                              2007019694

Design by Hernan Bonomo
Printed in the USA

 **IDEBATE Press Books**

Contents

Introduction

International Debate Education Association (IDEA) believes that free and open discussion is essential to the establishment and preservation of open, democratic societies, and its work supports initiatives promoting excellence and innovation in formal and informal education. IDEA cooperates and maintains contact with educational institutions in over 40 countries. It has extensive experience in conducting teacher training at all levels as well as organizing public speaking and debate events for secondary school students through workshops, competitions, and educational institutes. To complement these activities, IDEA has consistently produced quality curricula and educational resources.

Responding to the needs of secondary school teachers in many countries, IDEA has developed deliberative methodology (or deliberative education), which uses interactive teaching and learning approaches—role plays, simulations, debates, speeches, presentations, and so forth—to facilitate learning and create a new form of relationship between you and your class.

In an increasingly global world where our classrooms play host to students from a range of cultures and whose mother tongue is not English, it is imperative that teachers strive to teach and challenge all students regardless of their vast range of abilities and comprehension of English. This book provides lessons that allow teachers to teach a lesson that reaches all students, regardless of their present English-processing abilities. The lessons teach children "where they are" academically, and challenge them to reach higher levels of English-language comprehension and expression.

Deliberative education methodologies assist teachers in achieving a number of educational goals:

- Fostering interactive instruction, democratic dialogue, student-teacher partnerships, and cooperative learning

- Promoting student ownership of learning and application of knowledge

- Developing students' listening and communication skills

- Developing students' critical thinking and argumentation skills

- Developing students' research (traditional and computer) and critical reading and evaluation skills

IDEA is proud to present *Using Deliberative Techniques in the English as a Foreign Language Classroom*, the first volume in its series Deliberating Across the Curriculum.

Many of the lesson plans in this guidebook have been inspired by the sharing of ideas and experiences of teachers cooperating with IDEA in many countries. The author is grateful for all suggestions given and valuable input received.

How to Use This Manual

Integrating This Material into the Curriculum

Using Deliberative Techniques in the English as a Foreign Language Classroom is not a curriculum. It is a compilation of hands-on instructional approaches that helps you to teach your required curriculum in an exciting and thought-provoking way. Deliberative methodology provides an innovative way for you to bring subjects alive in the classroom. You can use the lesson plans as they are presented or you can modify them to fit your needs. For example, "You Oughta Be in Pictures" in chapter 4 uses a simulated casting session to help students improve their impromptu speaking skills. You could adapt it inputting imaginary scenes from a popular film or a film the students may have studied in class.

Goals

The goals of this guidebook are to use deliberative techniques to advance students in the following areas:

1. **Listening:** to enable students to understand spoken English in a variety of contexts at an advanced-proficient level

2. **Speaking:** to speak English at an advanced-proficient level in a variety of contexts

3. **Reading:** to read a variety of complex texts and comprehend their meaning

4. **Writing:** to develop skills in various types of writing—formal and informal, fiction and non-fiction

5. **Cultural/Social:** to use English in socially and culturally appropriate ways

Organization

Using Deliberative Techniques in the English as a Foreign Language Classroom is divided into five chapters:

- Chapter 1 defines deliberative techniques and discusses their uses and benefits in teaching advanced English speakers. The section presents the various components of the methodology—speeches and presentations, debate, role plays and simulations—and describes how you can use them in your existing curricula.

- Chapters 2 through 4 offer 20 detailed lesson plans using the various components as instructional formats.

- Chapter 5 discusses assessment and offers several rubrics to help you get started.

The book concludes with a glossary and a list of resources you can use to learn more about deliberative technologies and IDEA.

Lesson Map

This lesson map provides an overview of the lessons in the guide.

NAME OF LESSON	TYPE OF ACTIVITY	TIME (MIN.)	DESCRIPTION
■ INTRODUCTIONS TO SPEECHES AND PRESENTATIONS			
1. THE ATTRIBUTES OF SPEECH	SPEECHES AND PRESENTATIONS	45–60	Students present a portion of a historic speech.
2. ONE LESS LETTER	SPEECHES AND PRESENTATIONS	45	Students must write a story using fewer and fewer letters of the alphabet.
3. BUILD A STORY	SPEECHES AND PRESENTATIONS	60	Students tell impromptu stories based on a menu of the basic elements of a story: setting, characters, conflict, plot and resolution.
4. CHRISTMAS AROUND THE WORLD	SPEECHES AND PRESENTATIONS	2 LESSONS OF 60 MINUTES EACH	Students learn about Christmas customs around the world and quiz each other on what they remember.
5. GREETINGS VENUTIANS!	SPEECHES AND PRESENTATION	45–60	Students take turns explaining and demonstrating to visiting Venutians the various uses—real or imaginary—of ordinary objects.
6. THE STORYTELLERS	SPEECHES AND PRESENTATION	60–90	Students work in groups to write continuations of seven published stories.
■ INTRODUCTION TO DEBATE			
7. INTRODUCTION TO DEBATE	DEBATE	45	Students will learn the basics of debate through informal debate in which they are expected to present and defend their points to an opposing team.
8. MINI-DEBATES	DEBATE	60	Students will stage mini-debates on issues that are important contemporary topics in the United States.
9. OPEN FORUM	DEBATE	45–60	The class holds a group discussion during which students take turns presenting their own arguments and responding to arguments of others.
10. CORNER DEBATES	DEBATE	60	Students will listen to a statement on a controversial topic and decide if they agree or disagree with the statement. After meeting with a student on the opposing team and discussing their reasons for agreeing or disagreeing, they will be asked the question again and reassigned to a position team if necessary. They will then each have to take part in a debate in which they defend the position opposite to their belief.

NAME OF LESSON	TYPE OF ACTIVITY	TIME (MIN.)	DESCRIPTION
11. DEBATE AUDITIONS	DEBATE	3 CLASSES OF 45–60 MINUTES EACH	Students "audition" for a place in the Big Debate through elimination rounds of various debate speeches. The Big Debate will take place between the winning speakers from the previous day's auditions.
12. FLOW OF A DEBATE	DEBATE	45–60	This lesson uses a written debate to introduce students to the process of flowing debate.
	INTRODUCTION TO ROLE PLAYS AND SIMULATIONS		
13. GETTING TO KNOW YOU	ROLE PLAY AND SIMULATION	45–60	The lesson helps students develop the social skills needed when meeting someone for the first time.
14. WHAT AM I?	ROLE PLAY AND SIMULATION	45	The teacher tapes a concept word to the back of each student. The students must then circulate to find out what word they are.
15. YOU OUGHTA BE IN PICTURES	ROLE PLAY AND SIMULATION	45–60	Students audition for a role in a movie in which the scenes keep changing.
16. CULTURAL LESSONS	ROLE PLAY AND SIMULATION	45–60	This simulation involves learning how to read body language, gestures, and non-verbal language in different cultures.
17. AT THE IMPROV	ROLE PLAY AND SIMULATION	45–60	Students improvise a variety of situations in which they must solve a problem, work with a team, and/or think and act quickly.
18. PANEL OF EXPERTS	PRESENTATION AND ROLE PLAY	90 MINUTES FOLLOWED BY A 20-MINUTE WRAP-UP THE FOLLOWING DAY	On small panels, students pose as experts on a variety of things. After the students present mini-biographies of what makes them an expert, the audience is encouraged to ask the panel questions to "stump" them.
19. WRITE, READ, ACTION!	ROLE PLAY AND SIMULATION	2 CLASSES OF 45–60 MINUTES EACH	Students work in pairs to write detailed instructions of how to do common activities that other students then act out as the instructions are read.
20. SESSION OF THE SECURITY COUNCIL	ROLE PLAY AND SIMULATION	45–60	Students are involved in a role play of a session of the UN Security Council, focusing on resolving a fictitious conflict. They will research and present their nation's stand on the issue and then attempt to negotiate a possible solution.

Lesson Organization

Lesson plans follow a standard format:

Title

Instructional objectives

Description

Time

Materials

Preparation (optional)

Class layout and grouping of students

Procedure

Student products (where appropriate)

Assessment

Extensions and modifications (optional)

They provide detailed directions that help you avoid the guesswork typically associated with putting together a lesson.

So, if you are ready to get started, head to Chapters 2 through 4 and start browsing for a lesson plan. Once you teach using deliberative technologies, you will bring the excitement of learning to your English as a Foreign Language (EFL) students!

Chapter 1
Deliberative Education

Deliberative Education Defined

Deliberative education is a set of methodologies that employs speech, communication, discussion, and debate to maximize students' participation in the learning process. This methodology redefines the role of a teacher to more that of an educational coach confronting students with new tasks. Deliberative methodologies aim to do the following:

1. Engage students in the subject matter by providing an incentive to learn. This does not mean enticing your students with a reward but rather enticing them with an intrinsic desire to learn, debate, and build on that knowledge. You will see your students come out of a properly prepared debate exercise enthralled, excited, and ready to take on their next debate. They will be nervous and anxious before a debate and possibly during, but most students describe the feeling after a debate to be exhilarating and addictive. That's what learning should be!

2. Assist them in applying the knowledge they have gained to real world situations and dilemmas. Students want to talk about the world they live in, discuss issues, and understand how the changing world affects them. Deliberative education encourages students to gather insights and information about their society and use them to argue the issues and potential solutions.

3. Develop an array of skills—critical thinking, decision making, public speaking, and communication—that will enable students to adapt to the fast-changing realities of the modern world. Deliberative methodology puts students in situations—discussions and debates—in which they are expected to express their ideas and show their knowledge of a subject while challenging their opponents' message.

Deliberative education is a modern, innovative pedagogical approach that meets a number of educational aims:

1. It engages students in the subject matter by creating an atmosphere conducive to active learning. The traditional educational methodologies are based on a formulaic, top-down method in which students are passive recipients of knowledge passed to them by teachers. Deliberative education is based on dialogues between teacher and students as well as between students themselves. This methodology opens students to new ways of thinking; promotes independent study, problem solving, and the free expression of ideas; and encourages student creativity. By emphasizing personal investigation and respectful confrontation of different and often opposing ideas in the public but safe setting of a classroom, deliberative education constitutes an educational antidote to the development of passivity and authority dependence in students.

2. It encourages the application of knowledge. Students engaged in deliberative education become adept at applying knowledge they have gained in realistic discussions and debates. Traditional educational methodologies call on students to display their retention of knowledge through formal exams or tests to simply prove that they retained the information, whether it is useful or not. Deliberative education methodologies encourage students to reorganize their knowledge and apply it in different patterns depending on the context of the learning situation. Deliberative education has its roots in experiential learning, which involves a hands-on-approach to teaching and learning. In deliberative education, learners often develop knowledge through a series of experiential discoveries that they themselves direct through practical experience, which increasingly progresses in difficulty and thus increases knowledge. Deliberative methodologies prepare students for a variety of roles that they will be expected to assume during their adult life, and provide them with an array of skills necessary in many spheres in modern society, including private, social, and professional.

3. It encourages cooperation and teamwork. It shifts teaching and learning from teacher-centered to learner-centered activities. It raises the quality and the frequency of participation among students and encourages cooperation and sharing of the responsibilities for learning and its outcomes. This approach reflects the demands of the "real world," where individuals most often must work with each other to achieve their common goals.

4. It builds on different learning styles. By confronting students with different tasks, deliberative education meets each student's varying needs, abilities, and learning styles. Deliberative education responds to the needs of those students who focus on feelings and experiences. It responds to the needs of students who value observation and analysis, as well as students who are "doers" and focus on making links between concepts and their practical applications.

Deliberative education is especially useful in the teaching of social sciences, history, civic education, and languages—all subjects whose character and complexity of material require extended communication, discussion, and deliberation.

Deliberative Methodologies

The most prominent methodologies include debate and discussion, simulation and role play, and individual or group presentation. You can use these methodologies independently or in conjunction with each other. For example, a debate can lead to a role play or individual or group presentations. You can adapt each of these methodologies to different topics, group sizes, and educational goals. You may want to use a simulation exercise to introduce a unit and a role play or parliamentary debate to test students' knowledge at the end of the section. The options are numerous.

Educational debate

Educational debate is a formal contest of argumentation between two teams during which one team supports, while the other team opposes, a given proposition. A debate begins with a resolution, a simple statement about a topic that both teams subject to critical analysis. The team supporting the resolution speaks first and is referred to as an affirmative team (since it affirms a given resolution). The opposing or negative team must then refute the arguments offered by the affirming team and present arguments against adopting the resolution. Each team must not only outline their positions (the so-called cases) but also respond directly to their opponent's arguments. A neutral judge (either an individual or a group of individuals) listens carefully to the arguments of both sides and decides which team was most persuasive.

Debate is not only an educational methodology; it has been an intrinsic part of democratic institutions since the time of ancient Greece. The study and practice of debate furthers the development of skills essential for living in a democratic society. Because of its importance, academic debate is included in many educational systems (for example, in the United States, Great Britain, Australia), and thousands of secondary school students all over the world engage in debate activities in the classroom and in extra-curricular programs.

Debate is a flexible learning tool that meets a number of educational goals. It develops communication and speaking skills by providing students with an opportunity to deliver prepared presentations as well as to practice impromptu speeches in response to the arguments of others. Debate offers structure and imposes limits on speaking order and time, thus introducing an element of control that provides a framework for an organized exchange of ideas and that also serves as a reassuring support for beginners. It develops critical thinking and research skills and requires cooperation. Debate also is an excellent conflict resolution tool that emphasizes peaceful and tolerant communication and respect for the opinions of others.

Debate is best conducted over a number of lessons that focus on the individual processes involved—brainstorming and analyzing arguments, researching arguments in depth, preparing cases, debating the topic, and debriefing the debate—during which students evaluate their performance, consider the outcomes of the debate, and offer feedback to each other.

As a teacher, your role is best described as a coach and a facilitator. You should provide the students with a topic that engages their interest and has quality arguments on both sides of the issue. You should recommend or provide resources for researching the topic and offer guidance during the teams' preparation. You should also judge a debate and offer feedback after the debate is finished.

Although there may be only a small number of students engaged in the formal debate, the activity can involve the whole class. All students can research the topic, and those not on the teams can act as judges, assessing the debate and offering feedback to their peers.

Although debate is best used to assess what students have learned at the end of a unit, you can use it during any other stage of the educational process, including at the beginning of a unit to determine what students already know about a topic.

Role play

Role play is a technique in which students act out roles in a scenario depicting a problem, particularly one involving social life, for educational purposes. It is a planned interaction that involves realistic behavior under artificial or imagined conditions. It is an excellent tool for introducing students to different social roles.

The goal of this methodology is not only to practice competencies, but also to stimulate a discussion that allows students to identify effective and ineffective behavior under given circumstances. The technique has many variations—spontaneous role plays, dramatic skits, etc.—and involves any number of students. Role plays often involve fictitious characters, but you can also develop role plays involving current or historical figures.

Similar to other deliberative methodologies, role plays develop:

1. Communication skills: Role plays provide a practical illustration of what happens when people communicate, either verbally or non-verbally. They give students an opportunity to receive and provide feedback and help students develop active listening skills.

2. Research skills: Role plays help students develop their research skills by asking them to understand and support the views of their characters. Role plays enhance students' ability to critically evaluate sources through assessing information that other students present.

3. Problem-solving and critical-thinking skills: Role plays require students to generate ideas, respond to each other's views, propose alternative solutions, defend their views, and critique the views of others.

Role plays are highly engaging activities that increase students' participation both in the preparation process and during the activity itself. Role playing relies heavily on the experiences of participants in ways that increase their ownership of learning. Students are engaged in all stages of the role play, from planning through debriefing, and as a result are highly motivated to participate in the process of learning. This technique is very interactive and shifts teaching and learning from teacher-centered to student-centered. During the role play, you should exercise a minimum of control and intervene only to assure the smooth running of the lesson.

Role playing is also extremely flexible. You can change the role play while it is being conducted and fit the material to particular situations. Role playing can be brief or extended, although 45-minute role plays are most common. Similar to debate, a role play can be used during different stages of a particular unit. At the beginning of a unit, it can serve as an excellent introduction and illustration of a certain educational point or objective; at the end of a unit, a more complex role play serves as a closure or assessment of students' skills and knowledge.

Simulations

Simulations emphasize the big picture of experiencing group processes rather than focusing on the playing of an individual role of a certain character (although very often simulations are based on students playing certain roles). The difference between the role play and simulation is also in the authenticity of the roles the students take. In a simulation exercise a student is more likely to play natural roles—that is, roles that they sometimes have in real life. While in a role play, they would more often assume roles of fictitious characters.

Simulations develop the same skills as role plays and also provide students with an opportunity to do the following:

1. Increase their awareness of how their perceptions of others' motivations and cultural heritage can affect their interactions. Very often, good simulations will lead students to rethink their behavior and attitudes toward others.

2. Examine their own biases and focus on how their perceptions of differences can impact their interpersonal relations.

3. Understand how stereotypes develop, how barriers are created, and how misunderstandings among people are magnified. Students will also be able to observe, develop, and adopt appropriate mechanisms for successfully interacting with others.

Simulations are excellent teaching tools because they require active participation from students and develop strong motivation to learn. Simulation exercises also increase students' empathy and teach the rules of social interaction.

A well-developed simulation is also conducive to acquiring certain knowledge-based content, since it allows the participants to learn from personal experiences rather than from a lecture or even a discussion. For example, a cultural diversity simulation will make the participants much more sensitive to how cultural differences generate stereotypical perception and thinking than a lecture on the same subject. Many simulations also encourage the development of critical-thinking and problem-solving skills.

The drawback of this method, however, is that developing good simulations is labor intensive. A good simulation requires a well-conceived story line, plot challenges, and support materials for each stage of the simulation. The challenge in writing quality simulations is (a) in understanding that students will likely reach different conclusions and plans of action for each stage of the simulation and (b) in developing materials in advance to support the range of possibilities. In light of this, teachers new to simulation may be better off using already existing simulations and adapting them for their needs rather than developing them from scratch.

Presentations

Each of the methodologies discussed above involves student presentations, but you may want to include other types of oral presentations—readings, impromptu and prepared speeches, etc.—in your classroom as well. Deliberative education emphasizes developing presentation skills because students will need these throughout their lives and because presentations are helpful in achieving a variety of pedagogical objectives.

Is Deliberative Methodology the Best Way to Learn a Language?

Deliberative methodology challenges students to think, process, and analyze in English and put language to use—cementing language learning. Further, these methods engage students in a variety of cognitive and linguistic ways. It is the ideal way to approach advanced learners because they already know how to put words together to form thoughts and sentences. Language instruction should focus on context-rich materials presented in meaningful environments. It should encourage students to think, analyze, and construct arguments in the target language under a time constraint that forces them to abandon translating word for word and to internalize the target language. Using deliberative methodology enables you to provide the structure and format that encourage students to use this inner speech.

Deliberative methodologies provide significant practice in the skills of listening, speaking, and writing; they also refine argumentation skills for persuasive speech and writing. This expectation—which holds time restrictions for hearing and conveying ideas—allows students to think and argue in English, rather than merely produce rote sentences or presentations. This expectation is the key to transforming a learner into a fluent English speaker, as students now are decoding and encoding arguments in English. They simply aren't allowed the luxury of time to mentally translate from English to their native tongue for processing, comprehension, and developing a response, which they then translate back into English. They are taught to process information within the target language—the most significant benchmark to achieving fluency within a language.

Richard Nisbett, author of *Geography of Thought* (2003) agrees: "Debate is an important educational tool for learning analytic thinking skills and for forcing self-conscious reflection on the validity of one's ideas."[1]

---

1. Richard E. Nisbett (2003) *The geography of thought*. (New York Free Press, 2003), 210.

How Can I Fit These Types of Lessons into My Already Busy Teaching Schedule?

Deliberative methodology is an alternative way to teach; it imposes no additional content. You teach your regular curriculum using new, interactive ways to introduce the concepts and skills. For example, instead of lecturing your students about the Cold War, you might ask them to give structured presentations on the superpowers, have them role-play a UN session following the fall of the Berlin Wall, or have two teams debate the safety of the world before and after the Cold War. These experiences teach the same content, yet excite the students about learning far more than lecturing does.

Chapter 2
Introduction to Speeches and Presentations

Incorporating speeches and presentations into the curriculum compels students to use language in public speaking—a scary prospect for many people, but a skill they must master. Incorporating public speaking in the curriculum adds variety and fun to activities and encourages students to take risks and experiment with language while in the safe environment of the classroom. The activities here also encourage students to work together in pairs, groups, and on their own to develop a familiarity in working with others, and they allow students to build their knowledge base by helping others and being confident enough to ask for help.

Giving speeches and presentations is a part of being in the public eye, and doing so requires practice and familiarity to make the almighty stage a less scary place. Advanced- and proficient-level students will often face the prospect of presenting or making a speech whether in a debate, at a school function, or even at their best friend's wedding. Allowing them avenues in which to practice these necessary skills makes students more confident in their presentation and public-speaking abilities.

1. The Attributes of Speech

Instructional objectives

Students will be able to:

- observe and listen to how others use English
- focus attention selectively
- observe and model how others speak and behave in a particular situation or setting
- exercise voice volume appropriate to the situation
- review and give feedback on the work of others
- apply self-monitoring and self-corrective strategies
- hear and imitate how others use English
- use acceptable tone, volume, stress, and intonation, in various settings and with various audiences
- observe, model, and critique how others speak and behave in a particular situation or setting

Description

Students will learn the attributes of good speaking, using the transcript of a historic speech.

Time

45 minutes

Materials

The Attributes of Good Speaking resource sheet (for each student)

The Gettysburg Address transcript (for each student)

Audio version of speech

Preparation

Secure a copy of an audio version of the speech. You can easily download a digital copy read by actors by conducting an Internet search for "Gettysburg address audio."

Class layout and grouping of students

The students sit at their desks facing the front, from where one student will speak at a time.

Procedure

1. Distribute The Attributes of Good Speaking resource sheet and discuss.

2. Explain to the students that you will use Abraham Lincoln's Gettysburg Address to illustrate these attributes. Give the students some background on Lincoln and the speech. Teach the following points:

    a. Abraham Lincoln was the 16th president of the United States. Despite his current status as one of America's greatest, most beloved presidents, he was not universally admired during his presidency because the North and South were engaged in a brutal Civil War.

    b. The Battle of Gettysburg in the summer of 1863 was a turning point of the Civil War, during which the Union repelled the Confederacy's most ambitious invasion of the North. It was the war's bloodiest battle, with 51,000 casualties.

    c. Lincoln delivered this address at the battle site in Gettysburg, which he dedicated as a national cemetery. The main speaker, a man named Ed Everett spoke for over two hours. Lincoln gave this short address that became part of our history.

3. Distribute a copy of the Gettysburg Address transcript to each student and ask the students to read through the text briefly. Explain that you will now demonstrate good and bad examples of each attribute of a speech using the first two paragraphs. Read a few words of the text demonstrating one attribute and then have the students analyze your speaking by giving a thumbs-up or thumbs-down on your presentation. Note the portions and aspects that received thumbs down, and after completing your reading ask the students for suggestions on improving those aspects.

    Four score and seven years ago our fathers brought forth on this continent, a new nation, conceived in liberty, and dedicated to the proposition that all men are created equal.

    Now we are engaged in a great civil war, testing whether that nation, or any nation so conceived and so dedicated, can long endure. We are met on a great battlefield of that war. We have come to dedicate a portion of that field, as a final resting place for those who here gave their lives that that nation might live. It is altogether fitting and proper that we should do this.

4. Give the class three minutes to review the speech. When they are ready, explain that you will call out a student's name to read the speech from the beginning. That student must quickly come to the front of the class and, using excellent speech skills, present President Lincoln's speech as best she can. When you call out, "STOP!" you will say to evaluate a particular attribute, for example, "Class—Volume?" and ask students to give a quick thumbs-up or thumbs-down assessment of the speaker's volume. If she gets a majority of thumbs-ups, she may sit down, if not, she must continue the exercise until she does. You may evaluate a different attribute each time you call stop, or focus on one attribute until the speech is finished. Repeat the exercise until all students have had a chance to speak. If necessary, begin the speech again. The exercise should be fast-paced, with students moving between their seats and the front of the room frequently.

5. When everyone has had a chance to speak, you may choose to play the audio of the speech and analyze the eight aspects of speech listed above. If you do not want to listen to a prepared audio, do a final presentation of the text yourself, modeling excellent speaking skills.

Assessment

Students will receive feedback using the thumbs-up and thumbs-down assessment.

Extensions and modifications

Ask the students to write and present an impromptu speech on a topic you assign.

The Attributes of Good Speaking

1. **Body language:** includes proper posture, standing confidently—not leaning against a podium—and using your hands appropriately as you speak. You should refrain from looking disinterested or even terrified while you deliver your speech.

2. **Articulation:** speaking clearly. Your words must be distinct so that the audience can easily understand them.

3. **Pronunciation:** saying each word correctly and clearly.

4. **Word Choice:** using the correct words to make your point. Don't use slang, except to make a point. You should also be mindful to not repeatedly say, "You know . . ." or "Umm . . ."

5. **Pitch:** the highs and lows of your voice. Use inflection for variation and to emphasize a point. Avoid speaking in a monotone.

6. **Speed:** the pace at which you speak. Deliver the less important parts of your speech quickly while presenting the important points slowly so that the audience can understand and remember them.

7. **Pause:** a break in speaking for emphasis. When you want to highlight a word or emphasize a point, pause for a second before speaking. You can add extra emphasis by pausing before and after the important word or point.

8. **Volume:** loudness. Project your voice so that even those in the last row can hear. If you will be using a microphone, practice beforehand so that you know what volume is right. When delivering your speech, raise your volume to emphasize a point.

9. **Quality:** the way your voice sounds to others. Ask others what they think of your voice or record it for an idea of how you sound.

10. **Variation:** changes in pitch, volume, and speed. Change these at least once every 30 seconds, if only for just one word. Never go more than one paragraph without a change. Breathe life into your words by speaking them with meaning and character.

THE GETTYSBURG ADDRESS

Four score and seven years ago our fathers brought forth on this continent, a new nation, conceived in liberty, and dedicated to the proposition that all men are created equal.

Now we are engaged in a great civil war, testing whether that nation, or any nation so conceived and so dedicated, can long endure. We are met on a great battlefield of that war. We have come to dedicate a portion of that field, as a final resting place for those who here gave their lives that that nation might live. It is altogether fitting and proper that we should do this.

But in a larger sense, we cannot dedicate—we cannot consecrate—we cannot hallow—this ground. The brave men, living and dead, who struggled here, have consecrated it, far above our poor power to add or detract. The world will little note, nor long remember, what we say here, but it can never forget what they did here. It is for us the living, rather, to be dedicated here to the unfinished work which they who fought here have thus far so nobly advanced. It is rather for us to be here dedicated to the great task remaining before us—that from these honored dead we take increased devotion to that cause for which they gave the last full measure of devotion—that we here highly resolve that these dead shall not have died in vain—that this nation, under God, shall have a new birth of freedom—and that government of the people, by the people, for the people, shall not perish from the earth.

ABRAHAM LINCOLN
GETTYSBURG, PA
NOVEMBER 19, 1863

2. One Less Letter

Instructional objectives

Students will be able to:

- follow oral and written directions
- select, connect, and explain information
- apply self-monitoring and self-corrective strategies
- create a writing passage using critical thinking and a broad range of vocabulary
- describe the elements of a story
- create a story using essential elements

Description

Students must write a story using fewer and fewer letters of the alphabet.

Time

45 minutes

Materials

5 different colored pens or pencils (for each pair of students)

Dictionaries and thesauri

Elements of a Story resource sheet (copy for each student)

Preparation

Choose a topic of interest to your class and write it on the blackboard before class begins.

Class layout and grouping of students

Students will work in pairs.

Procedure

1. List the elements of a story: setting, characters, plot, conflict, and resolution. Distribute Elements of a Story and discuss. Explain how each element is essential for the next element to work. For example, without establishing a setting, characters cannot be introduced, and the conflict cannot exist without characters to bring it to life. The plot and

conflict rely on each other, as the plot is the sequence of events and the conflict is the problem to be solved. Without a plot, a conflict cannot exist, because it is a part of the plot. Without a conflict, there is no plot or sequence of events to tell. Finally, without a conflict, there can be nothing to resolve.

2. Tell the students that they will be writing a creative story—either fictional or based on events—about the topic on the blackboard. They are to include.

3. Explain that there is a catch: to prevent them from overusing letters, you have come up with a new rule. You will periodically call out, "STOP!" and announce a letter that they may not use from that point forward. They cannot use words that contain the now-eliminated letter and must find substitutes. They can use a dictionary and thesaurus to help them. When a new letter is eliminated, they must use another color pen or pencil. Remind them that the exercise is cumulative: they also must not use any letter that was previously excluded.

4. Read the following example slowly so that they can focus on your words and listen for any letter violations. Ask them to call out when they hear a letter violation.

I love to eat pizza. It is so tasty. The other day, my friend asked me to join her for a pizza at the new pizzeria in town. Yes!! I ordered a monster size with extra mushrooms, cheese, pepperoni and anchovies. I ate so much, I was in pain and had to drive my Mazda with the seat pushed all the way back to make room for my belly.

STOP—No Z

Well, with that much of the good stuff in my belly, I couldn't do much except wait for it all to digest. I headed to the movie theatre where I bought a ticket to see the new release of the movie with Catherine Jones and Antonio Banderas—the one where the guy with the mask makes a letter that is now forbidden with his sword. Very cool movie.

STOP—No Z or T

So I go in and find a place to relax. I like go in back—no chance—inside is dark and packed. Bummer. I find a place on an aisle and relax. Previews begin and everyone is noisy. Finally my movie begins!

STOP—No Z or T or A

I love movies! I love Ms. Zeta-Jones! I'm in love!

The students should have called out a rule violation for the last section: "Zeta" contains a "z," a "t," and an "a"—all forbidden.

5. Tell the students that as letters are eliminated, they will find the exercise increasingly difficult, but that they must continue to write in complete, coherent sentences. Remind them that the changes in ink or pencil color indicate when you introduced a new letter elimination.

6. Answer any questions the students may have and then organize them in pairs (in order to share the pens or pencils—NOT to share writing). Tell them where they can find a dictionary or thesaurus if needed and ask them to begin.

7. Every five or six minutes, call out "STOP!" eliminate a letter, and remind the students to change pens. Write the eliminated letter on the blackboard. Use the chart below to adapt the exercise to the skill level of your class. The letters progress from left to right

from "most frequently used letters as found in the most common words in the English language" to "least frequently used in the most common words in the English language."[2] E is the most frequently used; Q is the least.

E A R I O T N S L C U D P M H G B F Y W K V X Z J Q

8. Stop when you think the students have exhausted their vocabulary and ask the students to exchange stories with their partners to see if they have violated any letter elimination rules.

9. Ask individual students to volunteer to read their stories aloud to share ideas for new vocabulary in light of the letter eliminations.

10. Have students turn in their stories.

11. Start a new round by writing a new topic on the blackboard. They can use all the letters again until letter eliminations begin.

Student Products

Short stories abiding by the rules of letter elimination

Assessment

Pairs will informally evaluate each other. Formally assess stories on letter elimination, broader vocabulary use, and inclusion of the elements of a story in their writing.

Extensions and modifications

1. Have students present short, impromptu speeches. Occasionally call out a letter elimination and ask them to speak without using that letter.

2. Read excerpts from Mark Dunn's *Ella Minnow Pea* (MacAdam/Cage Publishing, 2001) about how the town lived with increasingly fewer letters.

2   http://www.askoxford.com/asktheexperts/faq/aboutwords/frequency. Retrieved January 3, 2006.

Elements of a Story

The following are five elements of a story. Each element depends on the others to exist in a story, and each element presented occurs in the order below.

SETTING

The time and location in which a story takes place. Other factors involved in setting include weather conditions, social conditions, and mood or atmosphere. These all can form the foundation from which a story can be told.

CHARACTERS

The people in a story.

CONFLICT

The opposition of forces that ties one incident to another and makes the plot move. Conflict is not merely limited to open arguments, rather it is any form of opposition that faces the main character.

PLOT

How events in the story are arranged to develop the basic story or the sequence of events in a story.

RESOLUTION

The final outcome of events in the story.

3. Build a Story

Instructional objectives

Students will be able to:

- observe and listen to how others use English
- negotiate and manage interaction with other learners to accomplish tasks
- select, connect, and explain information
- review and give feedback on the work of others
- formulate and ask questions
- evaluate one's own success in a completed learning task
- practice variations for language in different social and academic settings
- respond to the work of peers and others in writing
- use acceptable tone, volume, stress, and intonation, in various settings and with various audiences

Description

Students tell impromptu stories based on a menu of the basic elements of a story: setting, characters, conflict, plot, and resolution.

Time

60 minutes

Materials

Build a Story Menu activity sheet (copy for each student and the teacher)

Peer Evaluation activity sheet (copy for each student)

Class layout and grouping of students

Students will work in groups of four.

Procedure

1. Review the elements of a story: setting, characters, plot, conflict, and resolution.

2. Organize the students into groups of four and distribute Build a Story Menu to each student. Tell the students that they will be crafting an impromptu story by choosing dif-

ferent options from each section of the menu. They may choose as many as they like from each section (they must choose at least one from each section), BUT just as they are expected to eat everything they order from a menu, they are expected to address each aspect that they select.

3. Review the menu briefly and instruct the students to check off what they like from each section. Explain that the plot section does not offer choices but rather is decided based on the choices they made for the other elements. Give them five to ten minutes to make their choices, during which you do the same on your menu.

4. Use the elements you have selected to illustrate how they will craft an impromptu story. List the elements and tell your story. Distribute the Peer Evaluation activity sheet. Closely review the sheet with the students and explain that they are to use it to evaluate each other's work. These evaluation sheets keep students focused on the story and help them to listen for the elements of the story and assess if they were included.

5. Give the students ten minutes to make notes and draft a simple outline of their story.

6. Once the outline is complete, give them five to seven minutes to draft their stories. Tell them that each student will have five to seven minutes to present his or her story to the group, and remind them to be as creative as possible. Caution them that their story must fit in the five- to seven-minute time frame because going over will result in points being deducted.

7. After ten minutes, ask the students to present their stories.

8. Have the members of the group take turns telling their stories. After each student tells his or her story, instruct the other students to fill in the Peer Evaluation activity sheet and include written comments on any three areas listed. They should especially address any areas where they gave a score of 2. Presenters should also fill out an evaluation sheet on their own presentation so that you have an idea of how they judged their own work.

9. After they have completed their evaluation sheets for a presenter, the students in the group should offer a verbal critique of the presentation. Each student should have at least one positive point and one area that the presenter could improve. Presenters may ask the evaluators questions to clarify why they rated them as they did. Remind the speakers to thank their evaluators once the process is complete.

10. After all students have completed the exercise, ask them to turn in the evaluation sheets and keep their speech outlines. Ask the class as a whole how they thought the storytelling and the feedback sessions went. Discuss how the feedback will help them in future presentations.

Student Products

Return the evaluation forms to the presenters after you have reviewed them. Students will also have the outlines of their impromptu speeches.

Assessment

Evaluate the students informally by walking around the room and listening to students as they tell their stories and as they give verbal peer reviews. Informally read through the students' evaluation forms and judge for appropriateness. Return them to the presenters for a record of the feedback.

Extensions and modifications

1. Have the students write their impromptu stories and revise using the suggestions their peers gave them.

2. Have the students write a formal story using the Build a Story Menu and formally prepare it for the class.

Build a Story Menu

Instructions: Welcome to the Build a Story Café, where you order as much as you like from the menu at no charge! However, you must use each item you order—so choose wisely.

In the menu below, check off as many items as you want under each element to use in your story. There is no limit, but you must choose at least one from each category. Since plot is the sequence of events, you will outline your plot based on the choices you made among the other elements of a story.

Setting

Where:
- ○ Country
- ○ Village
- ○ City
- ○ Mountains
- ○ Forest
- ○ Ocean/Lake/River
- ○ Desert
- ○ Another planet
- ○ _____

When:
- ○ Past
- ○ Present
- ○ Future

Character(s)

- ○ Girl
- ○ Woman
- ○ Boy
- ○ Man
- ○ Thing
- ○ Machine
- ○ Idea
- ○ Ghost
- ○ Animal
- ○ _____

Traits of each main character

- ○ Greedy
- ○ Too nosy
- ○ Know-it-all
- ○ Lazy
- ○ Pessimistic
- ○ Totally in love
- ○ Seeks revenge
- ○ Naïve
- ○ Clumsy
- ○ Lacks confidence

- ○ Foolish
- ○ Courageous
- ○ Resourceful
- ○ Imaginative
- ○ Kind
- ○ Generous
- ○ Clever
- ○ Loyal
- ○ Strong
- ○ Optimistic

Conflict

- ○ Caught stealing
- ○ Eats too much
- ○ Acts foolish
- ○ Told a lie
- ○ Saw or heard a secret
- ○ Lost something
- ○ Been captured
- ○ Under a spell or curse
- ○ Goes to forbidden place
- ○ Finds forbidden object

- ○ Has enemy
- ○ Is undervalued
- ○ Is unrecognized
- ○ Causes jealousy
- ○ Forgets something
- ○ Broke something
- ○ Does not like something
- ○ Needs something
- ○ Needs to escape or hide
- ○ Needs to rescue someone

Resolution

- ○ Has helper
  - ○ Magical
  - ○ Non-magical
- ○ Is courageous
- ○ Is resourceful
- ○ Is imaginative
- ○ Is kind
- ○ Is generous
- ○ Is clever

- ○ Is loyal
- ○ Is strong
- ○ Is optimistic
- ○ Is rescued
- ○ Is transformed
- ○ Discovers skill
- ○ Conflict not solved
- ○ Helps self
  - ○ Exercises cleverness
  - ○ Uses inner traits

Plot

Review your choices and make sure they make sense; above all, make sure you can create a story from the choices you have made. Once you are satisfied, write a very brief description below of the plot you have created based on your choices.

_____

_____

_____

_____

_____

_____

_____

_____

_____

_____

_____

_____

_____

_____

Conclusion

O   Refer back to original setting in some way and compare.

O   How has/have the character(s) changed?

Adapted from Heather Forest, "Story Arts" at http://www.storyarts.org/lessonplans/index.html.

Peer Evaluation

Name of Presenter: _____

Name of Evaluator: _____

Instructions: For each statement below, mark your evaluation of the speaker.

1 = agree, 2 = not sure, 3 = disagree

Setting

The speaker explained the setting in detail.	1	2	3
The description of the setting made sense.	1	2	3

Characters

The speaker explained the characters in detail.	1	2	3
The description of the characters made sense.	1	2	3
The speaker described at least one main character.	1	2	3

Conflict

The speaker made the conflict apparent in his/her presentation.	1	2	3
The conflict made sense.	1	2	3
The conflict was creative.	1	2	3

Solution

The speaker gave a solution that made sense.	1	2	3
The solution was well planned.	1	2	3
The solution solved the conflict.	1	2	3
The speaker ended his/her speech appropriately.	1	2	3

Delivery

The speaker spoke naturally.	1	2	3
The speaker made eye contact with the audience.	1	2	3
The speaker was comfortable.	1	2	3
The speaker did not add extra, unnecessary words like "umm" and "you know."	1	2	3

The speaker's posture was appropriate.	1	2	3
If the speaker used gestures, they were effective.	1	2	3
The speaker used appropriate pitch.	1	2	3
The speaker used appropriate volume.	1	2	3
The speaker used vocal variety.	1	2	3

Language

The speaker used idioms and slang only when appropriate.	1	2	3
The speaker used good word choice.	1	2	3
The speaker's story was easy to follow and understand.	1	2	3
The speaker used correct grammar.	1	2	3

Timing

The speaker spoke in the allowable 5- to 7-minute time frame.	1	2	3

Provide commentary on any three areas.

1._____

_____

_____

_____

2._____

_____

_____

_____

3._____

_____

_____

_____

Evaluator signature: _____ Date: _____

4. Christmas Around the World

Instructional objectives

Students will be able to:

- actively connect new information to information previously learned
- use written sources of information to support their oral presentations
- paraphrase, summarize, elaborate, clarify, ask relevant questions, and make relevant comments in conversation, debate, and simulations
- participate effectively in face-to-face conversations on assorted subjects
- describe or read about an unfamiliar activity or topic
- read and write about subject matter information
- share social and cultural traditions and values
- practice recall of facts and differentiate between many pieces of information

Description

Students learn about Christmas customs around the world and quiz each other on what they remember.

Time

2 lessons of 60 minutes each

Materials

Christmas packets (for each pair)—each packet should contain a copy of

> Celebrating an Australian Christmas resource sheet
>
> Celebrating an Ethiopian Christmas resource sheet
>
> Celebrating a Hungarian Christmas resource sheet
>
> Celebrating an Indian Christmas resource sheet
>
> Celebrating an Iranian Christmas resource sheet
>
> Celebrating a Nicaraguan Christmas resource sheet

Knowledge Gap activity sheet (copy for each student)

Creative Writing Rubric resource sheet (copy for each student)

Preparation

Review Chapter 5 if your class is unfamiliar with the procedure of using a rubric.

Class layout and grouping of students

Students initially will work in pairs and then work individually on the writing assignment.

Procedure

Day 1

1. Explain to the class that many countries celebrate the same holiday differently. While not everyone in a country celebrates each holiday, the people who do celebrate a holiday have similar customs. Many people around the world celebrate Christmas, and do so in different ways. This lesson focuses on Christmas celebrations in six countries.

2. Divide the class into pairs. Distribute one Christmas packet to each pair and tell the students not to look at the sheets until you have explained all the directions.

3. Explain that each sheet in the packet describes how people in a country celebrate Christmas. Each student in a pair will take one of the sheets, read it, and remember as much as she can. She has two minutes to do so. After two minutes, the students switch sheets, read the new sheet, and quiz each other on the information on the two sheets. They have three minutes to do so. They will then have 30 seconds to write down any details they may want to remember from the two sheets. They will repeat this procedure two more times, using the remaining sheets. Once they have completed the exercise, they will fill in the Knowledge Gap activity sheet to test their recall.

4. Answer any questions the students may have. Tell the class to begin. Announce, "TIME" when appropriate according to the schedule outlined above, and remind the students of the next step in the exercise.

5. After the class has completed the exercise, collect the Christmas packets. Distribute the Knowledge Gap activity sheet and give the students 15–30 minutes to complete it. They can use their notes (but not the original sheets) if necessary.

6. Tell them to hand in their completed sheets for assessment.

Day 2

1. Tell the students to assemble in the same pairs. Distribute the Christmas packets and give each student the Creative Writing Rubric. Tell the class that each student will write a short story about a character from one of the countries using the information from the handout. Remind them that they are to use the five important elements of a story: setting, character(s), plot, conflict, and resolution. Refer to the Elements of a Story resource sheet (p. 24) if necessary.

2. When the students have completed the assignment, ask them to exchange stories with their original partner and critique each other's work using the Creative Writing Rubric. They should make sure that the story contains all five important elements. Explain that you will also evaluate each of their stories using the same rubric.

Student Products

Completed Knowledge Gap sheets and written short stories.

Assessment

You can modify the Creative Writing Rubric so that you and your students can evaluate the short stories. Note that if your students are unfamiliar with rubrics, refer to Chapter 5 on the how's and why's of rubrics and a quick lesson on how to teach students to complete and read a rubric.

Celebrating an Australian Christmas

While sleigh rides and snowmen are unheard of during the warm and sunny Australian Christmas season, beach time and outdoor barbecues are common. Familiar traditions such as family gatherings, feasting on good food, and exchanging gifts are also part of the Christmas festivities.

1. Australians celebrate in the laid-back Aussie lifestyle, which calls for a minimum of fuss and a lot of fun.

2. It's summer in Australia in December. People plan beach or pool time and a barbecue or picnic instead of a formal Christmas feast.

3. As in other parts of the world, people invite friends and relatives to celebrate with them; getting together with family and friends is an important part of the season.

4. People are creative with their Christmas menu. They select a wide variety of items such as seafood, cold meats, pasta, and ice cream—anything they like. Often, they eat the main meal at midday, and it is very casual.

5. People get into the spirit by putting up Christmas bells and a Christmas Bush, a native plant with red flowers. They also display white Christmas flowers and other plants in their home.

6. If Santa can't make it because of the heat, children can expect a visit from "Swag Man," hauling gifts in his four-wheeler.

7. Some large cities have public Christmas events. For example, in Melbourne people gather to sing Carols by Candlelight on Christmas Eve. This tradition began in 1937 when a radio announcer saw a lonely woman listening to Christmas carols with a candle in her window.

8. People exchange gifts with family and friends on Christmas morning.

9. Attending church is also an important part of many people's Christmas tradition.

10. Because the British settled Australia, visitors can expect to find variations of British Christmas traditions.

Adapted from http://www.ehow.com/how_10772_celebrate-australian-christmas.html.

Celebrating an Ethiopian Christmas

Christmas is a major holiday in Ethiopia, where more than half of the population is Orthodox Christian. The celebrations occur on January 7, the day that Ethiopians celebrate the Feast of the Epiphany, instead of on December 25.

1. People set up a manger scene that includes the Three Magi. Legend has it that the king bearing frankincense was King Balthazar of Ethiopia.

2. People burn frankincense, which was traditionally a gift suitable for a high priest, or mix frankincense with spices or seeds to create different aromas.

3. People attend church services if there is a church nearby. The services, which can last for three hours, sometimes require that men and women sit in separate areas.

4. People sing carols and carry candles either during the service or afterward.

5. People prepare a feast that includes a main course, such as *doro wat* (a spicy chicken stew), *injera* (flat round bread), and homemade wine or beer. The injera is used to scoop and eat food, replacing utensils. The Christmas meal, which is served on January 7, involves major preparations that include the purchase and slaughter of an animal (typically a goat or cow).

6. Traditionally, an Ethiopian Christmas does not include a Christmas tree. However, Christmas trees, sparkles, and artificial snow have begun to appear in the capital city of Addis Ababa.

7. Ethiopians do not customarily exchange gifts, but some families give children new clothing as a part of the celebration.

8. Children play *leddat*, a game similar to field hockey. Two opposing teams use sticks with hooks on one end and a ball made from locally grown trees. The teams often represent different regions of the country, and the competition and rivalry between them can be fierce. According to tradition, when the shepherds heard about Jesus' birth, they played this game in celebration.

9. A common way to wish someone a Merry Christmas is *ye ganna baal.*

Adapted from http://www.ehow.com/how_10775_celebrate-ethiopian-christmas.html.

Celebrating a Hungarian Christmas

In Hungary, children await the arrival of the angels and Baby Jesus on Christmas Eve. After opening gifts, families enjoy a festive meal and attend mass together.

1. People celebrate St. Mikulas day on December 6. Children place their freshly polished shoes outside their door on the evening of December 5, when St. Mikulas will come and reward good boys and girls with a piece of fruit and some candy. Very bad children will receive a piece of coal or an onion.

2. On Christmas Eve, parents hide the Christmas tree in a separate room away from the children and decorate it with *szalon cukor* (a Christmas candy), candles, an angel, and a bell.

3. When the bell is rung, the children know that the angels have decorated the Christmas tree and that Baby Jesus has arrived with gifts.

4. The family gathers around the tree holding hands and singing "Menybol Az Angyal" ("Angel from Heaven"). They then open gifts from Baby Jesus.

5. For Christmas Eve dinner, people serve *borleves* (wine soup) and fish. They also serve Tokay, the Hungarian dessert wine, after dinner.

6. Many of the Hungarian Christians attend midnight mass on Christmas Eve.

7. *Kellemes Karacsonyt* means Merry Christmas in Hungarian.

Adapted from http://www.ehow.com/how_13057_celebrate-hungarian-christmas.html

Celebrating an Indian Christmas

In India, Christmas is primarily a religious holiday celebrated by the small Christian community. Only a very small percentage of Indians are Christians—most are Hindus or Muslims—but for those celebrating Christmas, it is a colorful holiday.

1. Christians in India celebrate Christmas with a lot of music and dancing. Christians light up their homes in a blaze of festive lights.

2. Many people decorate their floors for the holiday with brightly colored powders and chalks. They sometimes use turmeric powder, paprika, and flour to "paint" traditional Christmas symbols such as angels and stars on the cement.

3. Indians decorate mango trees or any other tree-like plant from their gardens as their official Christmas tree.

4. In Goa, the trunks of palms are decorated with chains of light. In Kashmir, Christians paint bells with bright colors and make Christmas tree balls out of papier-mâché. They also make beautiful stars out of gold and silver foil.

5. In southern India, people make little lamps out of clay and place them around the house and on their roofs.

6. On Christmas, children receive presents from their parents, and employees receive presents at work.

7. In some parts of India the head of the household receives a lemon on Christmas morning. This is meant as a gesture of admiration and blessing from the family.

8. On Christmas Eve, Christian families gather in their inner courtyards, which are open to the sky. There they hold candles as the Christmas story is read. Afterward they set fire to a heap of dried thorns in a corner of the courtyard. They believe that if all the thorns burn down, the family will have good luck for the next year.

9. Catholics have midnight mass in their churches. This mass lasts for two or three hours and includes a lot of singing and dancing.

Adapted from http://www.global-christmas.com/scripts_en/world/asia/main_india01.html

Celebrating an Iranian Christmas

During the holiday season, Iranians celebrate Christmas twice! Since the majority of Iranians are Muslim, the only people that celebrate Christmas are two ethnic groups that are Christian—the Assyrians and the Armenians. Throughout history, Armenians and Assyrians were close; they have a lot of common points in the culture, ritualism, and life and manners. It should be noted that Assyrians are the last ethnic group in the world that still speak Aramaic—the language that Jesus spoke over 2,000 years ago.

1. Assyrians have their big Christmas celebration on December 25, while Armenians wait until January 6. However, both groups recognize each of the days as a special religious holiday.

2. January 6 is known as the Epiphany. This is the day that the Three Wise Men were believed to have come from Iran to Bethlehem to visit the Baby Jesus.

3. Many Christians set up a Nativity scene in their home and decorate a Christmas tree.

4. On December 1, Assyrian people observe a "Little Fast" in which they do not eat animal products—meat, eggs, milk, and cheese. This fast lasts through the end of the Christmas Eve mass, when the church bells ring and signal the end of the fast.

5. Assyrian people break the fast on Christmas Day with the "Little Feast," a Christmas dinner of *harasa* (chicken stew) as well as *abgusht* (a meat soup) and *tarcheen* (a chicken and rice dish).

6. The church is decorated with candles and lamps for Joseph, who lit candles to keep Mary warm during the birth.

7. Assyrian people give their children new clothes, which they wear on Christmas Day. Adults also wear new clothes that they bought for the occasion on Christmas Day.

8. While Iranian children don't receive typical Christmas presents, they do sometimes receive money at Christmas.

Adapted from http://www.ehow.com/how_11724_celebrate-iranian-christmas.html.

Celebrating a Nicaraguan Christmas

Many people in Nicaragua come from a mixture of Spanish and Native American cultures. Nicaraguans often weave age-old traditions from these cultures into their own Christmas celebrations.

1. People participate in Las Posadas, which is a nine-day reenactment of Mary and Joseph's search for an inn in Bethlehem.

2. People spend the weeks before Christmas stocking up on gifts, such as Nativity pictures, candles, and toys.

3. On December 7 people celebrate La Griteria, a festival honoring and thanking the Virgin Mary. Young people go from house to house yelling, laughing, and singing for the Virgin. People hand out traditional candies, fruit, sugar cane, and small plastic items when the crowd arrives.

4. At Christmas, children bring bouquets of flowers to the altar of the Virgin Mary in church.

5. People are called to attend Midnight Mass on Christmas Eve when the bells ring.

6. People follow Midnight Mass with a meal they've prepared themselves. Many people kill their own chickens and grow their own rice for the feast. They also serve favorite foods such as chicken tamales, *ensalada de jicama y naranja* (jicama and orange salad), *chile relleno* (stuffed chiles), and homemade sweets.

7. People then open gifts and set off fireworks as part of the celebration.

8. People also celebrate the feast of Epiphany on January 6. In Nicaragua, this holiday incorporates the legend of an old woman who turned down an offer to accompany the Three Wise Men to Bethlehem to see Jesus. Now she wanders the Earth looking for Him. The Three Wise Men often bring presents to children on this day.

9. People greet each other by saying, *Feliz Navidad*, which means Merry Christmas.

Adapted from http://www.ehow.com/how_11726_celebrate-nicaraguan-christmas.html.

Knowledge Gap

Name: _____

Complete the statements below with knowledge you gathered in your pair work. Work alone, and DO NOT refer back to the handouts for information. This is an exercise to test your recall of facts.

I have learned information by reading or testing my partner about how _____ is celebrated in 6 different countries. These countries were _____, Iran, _____, Hungary, _____ _____, and _____.

Let me tell you a bit about them.

1. La Posada is celebrated in _____ and takes ____ days, during which the people reenact Mary and Joseph looking for a place to stay. People attend Midnight Mass when _____. For La Griteria, which is held on December _____, the children shout and scream happily in honor of Mary.

2. In the country of _____, people decorate their houses with many bright lights and also decorate their floors with _____. Families gather in their home's courtyard to burn _____. If these all burn to the ground, they will have _____ luck the next year. The head of the house receives a _____, which means _____ _____.

3. St. Mikulas Day is celebrated on _____ in the nation of _____. Good children receive treats in their shoes while bad children receive coal or an _____. The Christmas tree is not decorated until _____ and it is hidden from _____ __. When everyone sees the tree, they gather around it and sing "Menybol Az Angyal," which in English means _____.

4. The Three Wise Men were said to have lived in _____ when Jesus was born. To honor this, the people here begin a Little Fast on December _____ where they refuse to eat any _____. The fast lasts until _____ when the people have a Little Feast complete with harasa. The big difference is that in this country, people _____ _____ gifts but children do wear _____ on Christmas Day.

5. More than half the population in _____ is Orthodox Christian and so celebrates the Feast of the Epiphany on _____ instead of celebrating Christmas on December 25. This country claims that one of the Three Kings came from here. His name was King _____, and he brought the gift of _____ to Baby Jesus. The people make delicious food including doro wat and _____, which is a type of flat pancake used to scoop food. Just like another country I read about, people do not exchange gifts but children _____ from their parents.

6. In the nation of _____, summer is in full swing and there is no snow at Christmas! Sometimes it is too hot for Santa to come, so children expect _____ to visit driving his _____. On Christmas Eve, the city of _____ holds Carols by Candlelight on Christmas Eve, when people come together and sing.

Creative Writing Rubric

	4	3	2	1	
Organization	Information is in logical sequence, which reader can follow with interest.	Student presents information in logical sequence, which reader can follow.	The piece jumps around causing the reader difficulty in following story.	Sequence of information is too difficult to follow.	____
Content Knowledge	Student demonstrates full knowledge.	Student is at ease with content and creativity but fails to elaborate fully.	Student is uncomfortable with content and is able to only state basic concepts.	Student does not have grasp of information; student cannot answer questions about subject.	____
References to information sheets	Work uses multiple references creatively and correctly.	Work uses more than two references creatively and correctly.	Work uses one reference or uses more than one reference incorrectly and without creativity.	Work displays no references. Work displays zero creativity.	____
				Total---->	

5. Greetings Venutians!

<table>
<tr><td>

Instructional objectives

Students will be able to:

- use responsive listening
- negotiate and manage interaction with other learners to accomplish tasks
- assess one's own success in a completed learning task
- interpret and respond appropriately to non-verbal cues and body language
- elaborate and extend other people's ideas and words
- select, connect, and explain information
- think creatively and critically

</td></tr>
</table>

Description

Students take turns explaining and demonstrating to visiting Venutians the various uses—real or imaginary—of ordinary objects.

Time

45–60 minutes

Materials

box of assorted gadgets, trinkets, everyday items (such as a mixer, a book, a stapler, a hubcap, a light bulb, a shoe, a safety razor, a key, a coffee cup, a camera, a toy—anything!)

sock

Preparation

Lay out the everyday items you have brought at the front of the room so all the students can see them.

Class layout and grouping of students

Initially, students will remain in their usual seats. When it is time to separate the Venutians and the Earth Greeters, organize the desks so that the two sides face each other.

Procedure

1. Explain to the students that they will take turns being either a Venutian (an alien from Venus) or an official Earth Greeter. The Venutians have just landed on Earth, and everything is very strange to them. They must learn how to use simple objects to survive, but they understand only basic English. The Earth Greeters will explain and demonstrate the use of these objects.

2. Ask the students to think of as many uses as possible for each item you have displayed and list these on a sheet of paper. Stress that the use can be real or imaginary. For example, hold up a sock. Demonstrate each use as you tell the students what a sock can be used for:

   a. a covering to keep a foot warm

   b. an ear warmer

   c. an oven mitt

   d. a puppet

   e. a scarf for gnomes

   f. a big teabag—put loose tea inside and soak in hot water

   g. a food strainer

   Give the class five to seven minutes to complete the assignment. Encourage them to be as creative as possible.

3. Once they have completed the assignment, divide the students into two groups. Tell one group that they are Venutians and ask them to move to one side of the room. The other group, the Earth Greeters, should move to the opposite side of the room, bringing their lists with them.

4. Welcome the Venutians to Earth and tell the aliens that the Earth Greeters will describe how to use several everyday items. The Greeters know that the Venutians can understand only basic English, so if the Greeters use words that are too advanced or confusing, the Venutians should ask them to simplify their vocabulary. Remind the Earth Greeters that they are to use the most basic English possible to explain the items and that they cannot abandon an explanation because they are having difficulty finding the appropriate words. They can use body language or ask teammates for help if necessary. Finally, remind the Venutians that they should not be too hard on the Greeters because they will be Earth Greeters next!

5. Hold up one of the items. Call out a student's name from the Earth Greeters group and ask that student to describe and demonstrate its uses. If another Greeter thinks of another use, he or she must call out, "ALTERNATIVE," and explain and demonstrate that use. This continues until the Earth Greeters have no further uses for that item. Then, choose another item, and repeat the process.

6. After the Earth Greeters have explained half the items, call out, "SWITCH!" and ask the Earth Greeters and Venutians to trade roles. Reiterate the rules and proceed as above until the Greeters have explained all the items.

7. Ask the students to return to their seats and facilitate a discussion of what they liked and didn't like about the exercise. Why was it so difficult to speak to someone with limited English? How did it change their presentation?

Student Products

Clever uses for everyday items

Assessment

You can informally assess the students by observing how they rephrase their explanations when someone does not understand them.

Extensions and modifications

Divide the class into pairs or groups. When a group or pair is called to demonstrate or explain an item's use, one student acts as the translator and must make up a narration while another student demonstrates the item's use.

6. The Storytellers

Instructional objectives

Students will be able to:

- negotiate and manage interaction with other learners to accomplish tasks
- use written sources of information to support their oral presentations
- request and provide clarification to their ideas and those of others
- elaborate and extend other people's ideas and words
- select, connect, and explain information
- use context to get meaning of new vocabulary and ideas
- use a variety of writing styles appropriate for different audiences, purposes, and settings
- experiment with variations of writing

Description

Students work in groups to write continuations of seven published stories.

Time

60–90 minutes

Materials

Story Starter packets (for each group). Each packet should contain the following:

    7 Storyboard activity sheets

    Story Starters 1–7 resource sheets

    42 blank sheets of writing paper

paper clips or stapler

blank Storyboard activity sheet

Preparation

Prepare the Story Starter packets for each group. Assemble a blank Storyboard sheet on top of a copy of one of the seven Story Starter resource sheets. Then add six blank sheets of writing paper in back of the Story Starter and staple or clip together. Write the story number in bold on the Storyboard sheet. Repeat for the remaining six Story Starters and clip the sheets together to form a packet.

If you cannot arrange your class into even groups of seven, adjust the group numbers so that you have groups with equal numbers. Distribute only as many Story Starters to each group as there are students in a group.

Class layout and grouping of students

The students arrange their desks in circles of seven.

Procedure

1. Tell the students that they are to work in groups to create a continuation and an alternative ending for several classic stories.

2. Organize the students into groups of seven and ask the groups to arrange their desks in circles. If the class does not divide evenly, make as many groups of seven as you can and place the extra students in a smaller group.

3. Review the key elements of a story—setting, character, plot, conflict, and resolution—and provide examples of each from any popular story that your students would know. Use a blank Storyboard to list the elements or list the elements on the blackboard for all to see.

4. Tell the groups that each member will receive a different Story Starter. They are to read it, fill in any information they can on the attached Storyboard activity sheet, and write a continuation. When you call, "TIME," they are to pass their stories to the person on their right, who repeats the process. This process continues until all members of the group have written part of each story. The last writer is to sum up the story's loose ends and supply an appropriate ending. Tell the students that although they may know the plot of some of the stories, their continuation and ending should differ from the original. The intent is not to duplicate a famous story but to create alternative plots and endings.

5. Review the function of the Storyboard sheets in the exercise. They give students an overview of the story and allow them to keep track of the elements as they read the Story Starter and the material that the other students have added. Stress that adding to the Storyboard is particularly important when they introduce new characters or plot twists.

6. List the rules for the students:

   a. Spelling does not count, as long as the other members of the group can understand what you wrote.

   b. List your initials or last name in the right-hand margin before beginning a continuation of a story.

   c. The final writers must tie up loose ends and conclude the plot.

   d. You will have five minutes to read the initial story starter and write your continuation. An additional minute will be added to each subsequent round to allow you more time to read the material that your classmates wrote.

e.   You will hear a thirty-second warning before time is up for each round. When you hear "TIME," you must stop writing even if they are in the middle of a word or sentence.

7.   Answer any questions that the students may have.

8.   Distribute a Story Starter packet to each group. Ask each member to take a different Story Starter and begin the exercise.

9.   After four minutes and thirty seconds, call, "Thirty seconds." After thirty seconds have elapsed, call "TIME." Make sure that all students stop writing.

10. Tell the students to pass their story packets, and write their initials in the margin below where the previous student stopped writing. Remind them to review the Storyboard sheet very briefly, read the Story Starter and their colleague's writing, and continue. They now have six minutes.

11. Repeat the process, adding a minute to each round. When the students have finished six rounds, announce that the next round is the last and that they must conclude the stories they received. They have ten minutes to complete their stories.

12. Instruct the students to pass their story packets to the right, so that they now have their original Story Starter.

13. Ask them to read silently the story in front of them and give them a few minutes to do so. Then ask the students to read their stories aloud to their group.

Student Products

Story packets with student and group-created stories

Assessment

You may assess students informally by listening in as they read the stories. You can also collect the stories and evaluate each student's writing, comprehension, understanding of story elements, and the writing process. If so, you may choose to use the Creative Writing Rubric on page 44 or create one specific to your teaching objectives (see Chapter 5 for more information). If you choose to formally grade writing through use of a rubric, give the students a copy of the rubric and review it before they begin to write.

Extensions and modifications

1.   Have all the students who started Story Starter 1 read their stories to the class. Do the same with the other stories. Compare the essential elements.

2.   Outline each student-generated story and have students use the writing process to improve their group stories through extra class sessions.

3.   Have the students guess the title of each of the original stories and compare the original plot with those of the students.

Storyboard

STORY #:

Setting (the time and place in which the story happens. Usually it includes descriptions of scenery, buildings, or weather to set the scene.)

_____

_____

Character(s) (a person or living thing who takes part in the action of a story)

_____

_____

_____

_____

Plot (a series of events and actions that relate to the conflict)

_____

_____

_____

_____

_____

_____

Conflict (the struggle between two people or things in a story. The main character is usually on one side of the central conflict. The main character may struggle against another important character, against the forces of nature, against society, or even against something inside herself, like feelings or emotions.)

_____

_____

_____

_____

_____

_____

Resolution (how the conflict is resolved in the story)

_____

_____

_____

_____

_____

_____

Story Starter 1

It was the best of times, it was the worst of times, it was the age of wisdom, it was the age of foolishness, it was the epoch of belief, it was the epoch of incredulity, it was the season of Light, it was the season of Darkness, it was the spring of hope, it was the winter of despair, we had everything before us, we had nothing before us, we were all going direct to Heaven, we were all going direct the other way—in short, the period was so far like the present period, that some of its noisiest authorities insisted on being received, for good or for evil, in the superlative degree of comparison only.

There were a king with a large jaw, and a queen with a plain face, on the throne of England; there was a king with a large jaw, and a queen with a fair face, on the throne of France. In both countries it was clearer than crystal to the lords of the States preserves of loaves and fishes, that things in general were settled forever.

Source: Charles Dickens, *Tale of Two Cities* (New York: Signet Classic, 1960).

Story Starter 2

If you really want to hear about it, the first thing you'll probably want to know is where I was born, and what my lousy childhood was like, and how my parents were occupied and all before they had me, and all that David Copperfield kind of crap, but I don't feel like going into it, if you want to know the truth. In the first place, that stuff bores me, and in the second place, my parents would have about two hemorrhages apiece if I told you anything pretty personal about them. They're quite touchy about anything like that, especially my father. They're *nice* and all—I'm not saying that—but they're also touchy as hell. Besides, I'm not going to tell you my whole goddamn autobiography or anything. I'll just tell you about this madman stuff that happened to me last Christmas just before I got pretty run-down and had to come out here and take it easy. I mean that's all I told D.B. about, and he's my *brother* and all. He's in Hollywood. That isn't too far from this crumby place, and he comes over and visits me practically every weekend.

Source: J. D. Salinger, *Catcher in the Rye* (New York: Barron's Educational Series, 1984).

Story Starter 3

The boy with fair hair lowered himself down the last few feet of rock and began to pick his way toward the lagoon. Though he had taken off his school sweater and trailed it now from one hand, his grey shirt stuck to him and his hair was plastered to his forehead. All round him the long scar smashed into the jungle was a bath of heat. He was clambering heavily among the creepers and broken trunks when a bird, a vision of red and yellow, flashed upwards with a witch-like cry; and this cry was echoed by another.

"Hi!" it said. "Wait a minute!"

The undergrowth at the side of the scar was shaken and a multitude of raindrops fell pattering.

"Wait a minute," the voice said. "I got caught up."

The fair boy stopped and jerked his stockings with an automatic gesture that made the jungle seem for a moment like the Home Counties.

The voice spoke again.

"I can't hardly move with all these creeper things."

The owner of the voice came backing out of the undergrowth so that twigs scratched on a greasy wind-breaker. The naked crooks of his knees were plump, caught and scratched by thorns. He bent down, removed the thorns carefully, and turned around. He was shorter than the fair boy and very fat.

Source: William Golding, *Lord of the Flies* (New York: Barron's Educational Series, 1984).

Story Starter 4

A few miles south of Soledad, the Salinas River drops in close to the hillside bank and runs deep and green. The water is warm too, for it has slipped twinkling over the yellow sands in the sunlight before reaching the narrow pool. On one side of the river the golden foothill slopes curve up to the strong and rocky Gabilan mountains, but on the valley side the water is lined with trees—willows fresh and green with every spring, carrying in their lower leaf junctures the debris of the winter's flooding; and sycamores with mottled, white, recumbent limbs and branches that arch over the pool. On the sandy bank under the trees the leaves lie deep and so crisp that a lizard makes a great skittering if he runs among them. Rabbits come out of the brush to sit on the sand in the evening, and the damp flats are covered with the night tracks of coons, and with the spread pads of dogs from the ranches, and the split-wedge tracks of deer that come to drink in the dark.

Source: John Steinbeck, *Of Mice and Men* (New York: Covici Friede, 1937).

Resource Sheet
Story Starter 5

I was born in the year 1632, in the city of York, of a good family, though not of that country, my father being a foreigner of Bremen, who settled first at Hull. He got a good estate by merchandise, and leaving off his trade, lived afterward at York, from whence he had married my mother, whose relations were named Robinson, a very good family in that country, and from whom I was called Robinson Kreutznaer; but by the usual corruption of words in England we are now called, nay, we call ourselves, and write our name, Crusoe, and so my companions always called me.

I had two elder brothers, one of which was lieutenant-colonel to an English regiment of foot in Flanders, formerly commanded by the famous Colonel Lockhart, and was killed at the battle near Dunkirk against the Spaniards; what became of my second brother I never knew, any more than my father and mother did know what was become of me.

Source: Daniel Defoe, *Robinson Crusoe* (Mineola, N. Y. : Dover Publications, 1998).

Story Starter 6

At the stroke of six Ikey Snigglefritz laid down his goose. Ikey was a tailor's apprentice. Are there tailors' apprentices nowadays?

At any rate, Ikey toiled and snipped and basted and pressed and patched and sponged all day in the steamy fetor of a tailor-shop. But when work was done Ikey hitched his wagon to such stars as his firmament let shine.

It was Saturday night, and the boss laid twelve begrimed and begrudged dollars in his hand. Ikey dabbled discreetly in water, donned coat, hat and collar with its frazzled tie, and chalcedony pin, and set forth in pursuit of his ideals.

For each of us, when our day's work is done, must seek our ideal, whether it be love or pinochle or lobster à la Newburg, or the sweet silence of the musty bookshelves.

Behold Ikey as he ambles up the street beneath the roaring "El" between the rows of reeking sweatshops. Pallid, stooping, insignificant, squalid, doomed to exist forever in penury of body and mind, yet, as he swings his cheap cane and projects the noisome inhalations from his cigarette you perceive that he nurtures in his narrow bosom the bacillus of society.

Source: O. Henry, *The Social Triangle* (Middlesex, England: Penguin Books, 1984).

When he was nearly thirteen, my brother Jem got his arm badly broken at the elbow. When it healed, and Jem's fears of never being able to play football were assuaged, he was seldom self-conscious about his injury. His left arm was somewhat shorter than his right; when he stood or walked, the back of his hand was at right angles to his body, his thumb parallel to his thigh. He couldn't have cared less, so long as he could pass and punt.

When enough years had gone by to enable us to look back on them, we sometimes discussed the events leading to his accident. I maintain that the Ewells started it all, but Jem, who was four years my senior, said it started long before that. He said it began the summer Dill came to us, when Dill first gave us the idea of making Boo Radley come out.

I said that if he wanted to take a broad view of the thing, it really began with Andrew Jackson. If General Jackson hadn't run the Creeks up the creek, Simon Finch would never have paddled up the Alabama, and where would we be if he hadn't? We were far too old to settle an argument with a fist-fight, so we consulted Atticus. Our father said we were both right.

Source: Harper Lee, *To Kill a Mockingbird* (New York: Barron's Educational Services, 1984).

CHAPTER 3
Introduction to Debate

Debate enables students to express their ideas in a safe environment, where they can have fun and experiment with a new language while being challenged by other students. It encourages students to take risks with language and to think and process in the target language—a sure way to improve speaking and listening skills dramatically. In debate participants voice their ideas and back them up with evidence. Debating involves research and teamwork and so accustoms students to work together. It allows them to build their knowledge base by helping others and gives them confidence to ask for help.

Advanced- and proficient-level students will often face the prospect of debating both in formal and informal settings. When they make a simple decision, such as what movie to see, or argue a very crucial topic, they are debating. Allowing them avenues in which to practice these necessary skills makes students more confident in their new language.

7. Introduction to Debate

Instructional objectives

Students will be able to:

- discuss differing points of view
- present and defend their viewpoints in a public structured setting
- focus attention selectively
- review and give feedback on the work of others
- apply self-monitoring and self-corrective strategies
- use acceptable tone, volume, stress, and intonation in various settings and with various audiences
- observe, model, and critique how others speak and behave in a particular situation or setting

Description

Students will learn the basics of debate through an informal debate during which they will present and defend their points to an opposing team.

Time

45 minutes

Materials

Debate Basics resource sheet (copy for each student)

Preparation

Prepare one or more arguments for students to debate.

Class layout and grouping of students

The students will work at their desks with a partner for the first 20 minutes. The second portion of the lesson involves half of the class standing at the front of the room on two opposing sides, with the remainder of the class at their desks as the audience. The final portion involves everyone at his or her desks in a discussion.

Procedure

1. Arrange the class in pairs and assign the students a resolution. Examples of appropriate beginner resolutions are the following:

    - Alcohol is addictive and should be illegal.

    - Curfews are necessary for people under the age of 18.

    - Arranged marriages should be banned.

    - Distributing condoms to minors encourages sexual activity.

    - The legal age to drive should be raised to 21—the same as the legal age to drink.

2. Tell the students that they will be debating one side of the resolution but that they will learn which side they are assigned only just before the debate begins. This means that they must prepare both sides. They will have the next 20 minutes to work with a partner to create a list of five arguments for and five arguments against the proposition.

3. After 20 minutes is up, choose 10–16 students randomly. Conform your group size according to the number of students in your class. You want to have two separate debating groups and an audience. If you have 20 students, for example, have 2 groups of 5 and 10 audience members. If you have 32 students, have 2 groups of 8 and 16 audience members. Ask the debating groups to come to the front of the room and move to opposite sides, while the audience remains in the middle.

4. Assign one group (the affirmative) to argue for the proposition and the other (the negative) against it. Tell them that they have 15 minutes (more if there are more than 5 students per side) to debate the resolution and that you will call out the time remaining periodically throughout the debate. During those 15 minutes, every person must share at least one of his or her points.

5. Explain to the students that often the other team will make a valid point with which they agree. They do not always have to dispute every argument but should acknowledge the argument and go on to make their point. For example, imagine that a person on the affirmative of the resolution "Alcohol is addictive and should be illegal" makes a compelling argument that alcohol can kill. She then asks a person on the negative if he agrees. If he does, he should say, "You may be correct, but everything in excess can kill—for example, too much oxygen in certain conditions can kill, but we can't make oxygen illegal, can we?"

6. Choose a student from the affirmative to start the debate. This is also known as the constructive speech. After she makes her point, she should call out the name of someone on the negative and ask that person, "Don't you agree?" The chosen person should directly respond to the question and then give a point from the negative argument. This is also known as a rebuttal speech. Once he has done so, he then chooses a person from the affirmative who hasn't spoken, and asks her, "Don't you agree?" This process continues until everyone has made an argument. Call out the remaining time periodically. Do not allow students to exceed the time limit.

7. After 15 minutes, ask the debaters to return to their seats. If this is the first time debating, review the debate and discuss how the students felt about the experience.

8. Choose another group of students and stage another debate as outlined above.

9. After both debates have taken place, have all the students be seated. Discuss the points that were made, the way that some people presented their arguments, and who made the most convincing arguments. Talk with the students about who the winning side was in each debate.

10. Distribute Debate Basics resource sheet and use it to explain the basic format of a formal debate. Explain that a formal debate has a more rigid structure than the debate the class just conducted. Describe the following elements of debate:

    a. Speaking order—see the diagram below.

    b. At least one judge watches a debate and records the points made by each side. In the end, the judge determines the overall winner.

    c. Each debate is timed by the chair, who is the moderator for the debate. The debate format determines the time allotted for each speaker.

11. Using the students' experience today as a model, show how their debate mirrored the speaking order presented on the resource sheet. Point to each person that presented and show the progression of the discussion and how it is reflected on the sheet. Also show how their placement in the classroom during the debate mirrored the debate format presented on the Resource Sheet.

Debate Basics

Organization

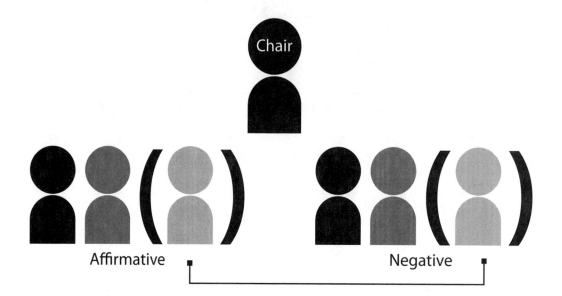

Affirmative   Negative

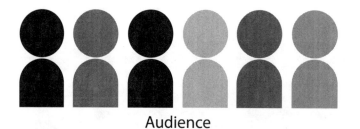

Audience

Speaking Order

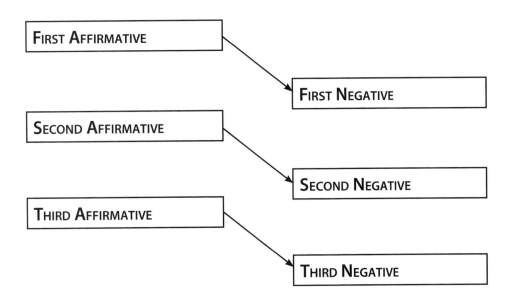

8. Mini-Debates

Instructional objectives

Students will be able to:

- demonstrate good comprehension during a variety of exchanges by responding appropriately to each other
- actively participate in small-group and full-class discussion
- actively connect new information to information previously learned
- work in teams to achieve common goals
- use written sources of information to support their oral presentations
- review and give feedback on the work of others

Description

Students will stage mini-debates on important contemporary topics.

Time

60 minutes

Materials

Judge Briefing Sheet (copy for each judge)

Debate Score Sheet (copy for each judge)

Should Boxing Be Banned? resource sheet (copy for each member of the group)

Imposition of Democracy resource sheet (copy for each member of the group)

Genetically Modified Food resource sheet (copy for each member of the group)

Should Smoking Be Restricted? resource sheet (copy for each member of the group)

Name tags or small pieces of paper and pins to attach to the students' clothing to indicate their role during the exercise

One stopwatch for each group

Preparation

Prepare a short outline of the mini-debate format on a flip chart or chalkboard. The format is as follows:

Affirmative Debater's Constructive Speech (4 minutes)

Negative Debater's Constructive Speech (4 minutes)

Affirmative Debater's Rebuttal Speech (4 minutes)

Negative Debater's Rebuttal Speech (4 minutes)

Feel free to add more speeches to accommodate the number of students in the class or to adjust for the class's ability level.

Class layout and grouping of students

Students will receive directions in their regular seating arrangement. They will meet in groups around the room to participate in the debates.

Procedure

1. Describe two key speeches in debate: constructive and rebuttals. Explain that constructive speeches take place during the first half of the debate because they construct or build the foundation for the round. This means that the constructive speeches establish what will be debated. The rebuttal speeches are given at the end of a round; this is the speech that summarizes arguments already made in a last attempt to convince the judge that your team should win the round.

2. Explain that you will divide the class into four groups. Each group will be assigned a debate topic and will be given a resource sheet on the topic. The issues are

     a. Should Boxing Be Banned?

     b. Imposition of Democracy

     c. Genetically Modified Food

     d. Should Smoking Be Restricted?

3. Explain that each group will be further divided into three teams: two teams will take opposing sides in the debate and the third will judge the debate and determine the winner. In this lesson, the judge will also serve as timekeeper.

4. Review the mini-debate format and answer any questions the students might have.

5. Divide the students into four groups of six and assign each pair in the group a role. Two will debate the affirmative, two will debate the negative, and two will judge the debate and determine the winner. (You may have to adjust the size of the teams to accommodate your class.)

6. Assign each group a topic and distribute the issue descriptions. Explain that these descriptions and arguments are taken from an on-line database of debate topics called Debatabase, developed by experienced debaters. Students may add arguments to those provided. Note that the sheets are simply a guide for those new to debating. If you think your students are capable and you don't want them to become too reliant on the argument sheets, ask them to develop their own points. Then allow them 30 seconds to quickly scan the sheets if they become "stuck" for points.

7. Allow the affirmative and negative teams 15 minutes for preparation. During this time, they should decide who on their teams will give the constructive and the rebuttal speeches.

While these students are preparing, distribute the Judge Briefing Sheet and Debate Score Sheets to the third team and instruct the judges on their responsibilities—what to look and listen for in a debate, how to assign points, etc. Remind the judges that they must be neutral and evaluate the quality of arguments presented in debates. They should not decide the cases based on their personal opinions and views on the issue. Finally, distribute the stopwatches and give the students a quick lesson on how to use them. Have the judges do a practice run on using them correctly. You may also choose to keep the time for all groups yourself.

8. Answer any questions the students may have about the issues or the assignment.

9. Write the following schedule on the board:

> Affirmative Constructive (4 minutes)
>
> Negative Constructive (4 minutes)
>
> Affirmative Rebuttal (4 minutes)
>
> Negative Rebuttal (4 minutes)

Explain that these are strict time limits that the debaters cannot extend. The judge for their debate will keep track of time, and their ability to stay within their time limits will be reflected in their scores.

10. If you are keeping time, call, "TIME." If the judges are keeping time, tell them to set the stopwatch as previously instructed, and tell the students to begin the debates. You should time the debates and ensure that each judge is also keeping time for the debate she is observing.

11. Once the debates are finished, give the judges five minutes to determine the winner. While the judges are working, debrief the debaters using the following questions:

    *   What were the most difficult aspects of the exercise?
    *   Which students had to argue the side they agreed with, which they disagreed with?
    *   What techniques did they use to persuade the judges?
    *   What would have improved the quality of the debates?

12. Ask the judges to announce their decision and provide a brief justification for it. Then debrief them using the following questions:

    *   What influenced your decision most (quality of the arguments, style of presentation, etc.)?
    *   Did your personal views on the issue make it difficult to judge objectively?
    *   What would have improved the quality of your judging?

Assessment

This exercise allows only for informal assessment through listening to arguments as you circulate. Listen to the judge's decisions and rationale to help further evaluate student comprehension.

Judge Briefing Sheet

1. You will hear a debate between two sides and you will be expected to determine the winner at the end of the debate. How do you determine who has won a debate? The team who does the better job stating their position and invalidating or refuting their opponent's position should win the debate.

2. The debaters are responsible for outlining their arguments and defending them in a manner that makes sense and gives reason to believe that their side is the correct one. Your job is to weigh each team's reasons and/or evidence against the other team's and determine who did the best job providing evidence that supports their position. Be careful not to let your personal opinion on the issue cloud your judgment of the debate. You are expected to judge simply on the evidence or reasons that are presented within the confines of the debate.

3. When the debate begins, keep time using a stopwatch or other timepiece like a wall clock with a second hand.

4. Speeches—each lasting 4 minutes— occur in the following order:

    > Affirmative Debater's Constructive Speech
    >
    > Negative Debater's Constructive Speech
    >
    > Affirmative Debater's Rebuttal Speech
    >
    > Negative Debater's Rebuttal Speech

    Take careful notes on each, recording the points raised and defended as well as the arguments each team uses in attacking the other team effectively.

5. Now review your notes and look at the arguments that were made. Consider the following in determining which team did the best job:

    a. When a team made a point, did they give adequate rationale to back it up?

    b. When the other team attacked a specific point, did the team defend the point when it was their turn to speak?

6. Using these considerations as you review your notes, make an objective decision as to who won the debate. Be sure your notes give you the evidence you need to defend your decision.   You will have to explain who you feel won the debate and why.

7. Finally, you do not want to appear biased as a judge. Try to say nothing at all throughout the debate. Try to be as neutral as possible; it is best to say nothing, take good notes, and appear interested.

Debate Score Sheet

Affirmative Team

Debaters' Names: _____

First Constructive   First Rebuttal

_____   _____

Negative Team

Debaters' Names: _____

Second Constructive   Second Rebuttal

_____   _____

As each debater presents, take notes in the appropriate columns below. Then after the presentation, give her a score between 1 and 30 (1 is lowest and 30 is highest) based on how you think he/she presented her case, defended her points, and effectively argued against the points made by the other team. This score should be listed on the lines above. A score of 10 might suggest that she did a poor job on these aspects, while a score of 20 suggests that she did a fair job with a few things they could have done better. A score of 23 or over would suggest that she did reasonably well on all aspects in the debate. List any comments in the columns below that you want to share with the debaters at the end of the debate.

_____   _____   POINTS   _____   _____

Comments for Affirmative:

Comments for Negative:

The team that did a better job in debating the topic was _____

Judge's signature: _____

2008 © International Debate Education Association

Should Boxing Be Banned?

During the last century, hundreds of boxers died in the ring or shortly afterward—the youngest recorded victim was just 12 years old. Thousands more, including one of the greatest fighters of all time, Muhammad Ali, suffered permanent disfigurement, detached retinas, and a whole host of neurological complaints. Despite a tightening of safety regulations, these injuries have continued. Yet efforts to ban the sport have failed.

PROS	CONS
Medical evidence suggests that even if a boxer survives individual bouts relatively unmarked, the cumulative effect of a career in boxing can lead to a greater susceptibility to diseases such as Parkinson's. Although the incidence of injury is much higher in sports such as basketball, the risk of serious injury in boxing is far greater. In fact, that risk is so great that boxing should be banned. A ban, quite simply, would mean fewer people dead, injured, or permanently brain damaged.	Boxers are aware of the significant risks of their sport and are paid well for accepting them. We allow individuals to engage in known risk behaviors—smoking and hang gliding, for example. Why should we single out boxing for abolition? Boxing authorities have made every attempt to minimize injury. Doctors and medical equipment are present at ringside, and referees intervene to stop fights if necessary.
Boxing is the only sport in which combatants intentionally injure each other. In the 21st century it is barbaric that we allow people to intentionally inflict injuries on others for the sake of public entertainment and private profit. People under 16 should also be banned from amateur fights because of the sport's health risks. It seems curious that in many countries you can start boxing before you are legally able to drive.	Most people who call for a ban on boxing have no understanding of the sport beyond a gut disapproval of it. Boxing's appeal lies in its simplicity, the distillation of the sporting contest to its most basic form—a physical battle between two egos. To say that boxing is the only sport where opponents intend to injure one another ignores the reality of sports like hockey. Introducing an age or fight limit may well be sensible, but there is no compelling argument for a ban.

PROS	CONS
Boxing is exploitative. An average boxer will compete in 30 to 40 professional bouts before his (or her) health and skills deteriorate dramatically. While it may well be in a fighter's interest to hang up his gloves, those around him have a financial incentive to push him into more fights.	A ban on boxing would rob many talented poor and working-class individuals of an opportunity to become rich and successful. Muhammad Ali was a sanitation worker who used his talent to become a global legend. When asked in a recent interview if he would do anything differently or if he had any regrets, his answer was a resolute "No." Many fighters accept their injuries as the flip side of the coin of success.
The celebrity awarded boxers glamorizes and legitimizes violence in society. Boxers are not role models of whom we should be proud.	Boxing is one of the least culpable in promoting negative stereotypes. Far more dangerous is the "sport" of wrestling, in which the violence is not part of a contest but a macho soap opera. Most boxing is on late in the evening anyway, and therefore its impact on children is less damaging than that of other sports.
Asserting that boxing would just "go underground" is not a valid argument. Dogfighting and cockfighting were banned to protect the welfare of the (admittedly, non-consenting) combatants. When these fights come to the attention of the police, the perpetrators receive hefty penalties. These penalties are an effective deterrent and would be for boxing also if implemented.	A ban on boxing would drive it underground, where fights would be unregulated, with no medical supervision. The safety of boxers should be paramount; to minimize the risk of injuries, it should remain legal but regulated.

Source: The content on this page is taken from Editors of IDEA, *The Debatabase Book*, 3rd. ed. (New York: International Debate Education Association, 2007). Adapted from IDEA's on-line Debatabase at http://www.idebate.org.

Imposition of Democracy

The U.S. invasion of Iraq has raised the question of whether imposing democracy by force is permissible—or even possible. Many believe that for democracy to be successful, democratic institutions must develop gradually along with various social and economic structures. Countering this stance is the example of West Germany and Japan, which, following World War II, had democratic regimes imposed by the Allies. Both countries have become stable democracies.

PROS	CONS
History has shown that democracy is the best form of government. Countries have not only the right but also the duty to intervene to liberate others so they can enjoy their human rights. Furthermore, because war between two true democracies is rare, the removal of repressive regimes promotes world peace.	Arguing that one nation can successfully impose democracy on another is untenable. Democracy relies on the rule of law (undermined by military imposition), freedom of choice and independence (destroyed by external determination), and accountability (impossible when a foreign power chooses one's rulers).
Merely pressuring dictators to move toward democracy is insufficient, and internal opposition is often too weak to compel reform. The international community cannot permit countries to shroud themselves in the pretense of free elections in order to gain international funding or to prevent invasion.	Encouraging democracy is not the same as imposing it. The desire for and fight for democracy must come from within; otherwise the political system will be unstable.
During the Cold War, Western powers often supported dictatorial regimes for reasons of realpolitik. This is inexcusable in the 21st century. Past complicity in dictatorships requires us to make amends by aggressively promoting democracy.	Turning on a regime that we once maintained is morally reprehensible. The 21st-century world is a dangerous place. Stability may be safer than universal democracy bought with many lives and at the price of massive resentment. The idea of democracy may be degraded in the eyes of many who associate it with invasions undertaken for suspect motives and the imposition of a culturally discordant polity.

PROS	CONS
Limiting those states that harbor and trade with terrorists would reduce terrorism. Preventive attacks on dictatorships thwart future attacks.	The doctrine of prevention depends on analyzing unclear evidence; undertaking potentially unjustified invasions will result in increased support for terrorists. "Security" is merely an excuse for intervening in oil- or resource-rich areas, while those in poorer nations are left to suffer.
Suggesting that people in various regions of the world will not accept the rule of law or protection for civil rights is fallacious. Democracy comes in enough forms to allow for social and historical variations—remember, illiberal political parties can always stand for election.	To impose democracy is to foist a set of Western values onto populations with different cultural backgrounds. Permitting the election of former dictators can lead to potentially serious problems in the future.
When a country is already engaged in conflict or civil war, intervention may help resolve the conflict. To wait, as occurred in Rwanda, will only permit carnage to continue longer.	Intervention may escalate the conflict. Democracy may be encouraged after a war has ended; dictatorships can be undermined by economic and cultural sanctions. Neither requires costly (in lives and money) military action.
To rely on multilateral action is utopian. The UN Charter does not permit intervention in the domestic affairs of independent nations, and in any case, some members of the Security Council are not democracies. Unilateral or bilateral action is the only realistic possibility.	Unilateral action is, in reality, dangerously dependent on the political whim of foreign electorates who are often unwilling to commit troops and money to long-term nation building. A bloody invasion and regime change, followed by anarchy when the external power swiftly withdraws, are far worse than a dictatorship. Even when invaders remain to oversee the installation of a new regime, they may choose pliant appointees rather than risk the uncertainty of true democracy.

Source: The content on this page is taken from Editors of IDEA, *The Debatabase Book*, 3rd. ed. (New York: International Debate Education Association, 2007). Adapted from IDEA's on-line Debatabase at http://www.idebate.org.

Genetically Modified Foods

The development of genetically modified (GM) foods has precipitated an ongoing debate among consumers, environmentalists, scientists, and even economists. On the one hand, genetic modification has improved crop characteristics—yield, resistance to disease, pests, and drought, etc.—and has contributed to global health. Recently, scientists announced the development of "golden rice"— rice genetically modified to produce greater levels of vitamin A—which can help prevent a variety of diseases in developing countries. On the other hand, the procedure has raised a number of concerns, including long-term risks to humans and the environment. Economists also point out that because biotechnology companies often patent GM crop varieties, farmers will become increasingly dependent on monopolies for seed.

PROS	CONS
Genetic modification is unnatural. There is a fundamental difference between modification via selective breeding and genetic engineering techniques. The former occurs over thousands of years and so the genes are changed much more gradually. With change occurring so rapidly, we now have no time to assess the long-term effects of these products on human health and the environment.	Genetic modification is entirely natural. The process of crop cultivation by selective breeding, which has been performed by farmers for thousands of years, leads to exactly the same kind of changes in DNA as modern modification techniques do. Current techniques are just faster and more selective. In fact, given two strands of DNA created from the same original strand, one by selective breeding and one by modern modification techniques, it is impossible to tell which is the "natural" strand. The changes resulting from selective breeding have been just as radical as those from current modifications. Wheat, for example, was cultivated through selective breeding from an almost no-yield rice-type crop into the super-crop it is today.

PROS	CONS
Introducing the DNA of one species into the genes of another is wrong. This attempt to play God is shortsighted and unnatural.	It is perfectly natural and safe to introduce genes from one organism into another. We must remember that all DNA is made up of the same four fundamental molecules regardless of which organism the DNA came from originally. DNA from all organisms is very similar. Human DNA is 99% the same as chimpanzee DNA and about 50% the same as grass DNA. Consequently, the addition of genes from one organism into the DNA of another is like using LEGOs to create a structure. Indeed such processes occur all the time in nature in sexual reproduction.
Testing GM food is often difficult. Biotechnology companies are often unwilling to submit their results for peer review. Furthermore, in some countries government agencies are often unwilling to stop GM foodstuffs from reaching the shelf because of the clout the companies have with the government.	This debate should be decided on the basis of hard facts, not woolly assertions and environmental sentiment. Until scientific tests show that GM food poses a risk to agriculture or health, it should not be banned. GM foods undergo extensive testing before they are placed on the market. This testing takes two forms: peer review by other scientists and testing by the food standards agencies in the countries in which the product is to be marketed. For example, in the United States all GM food must be tested for nine years before being released onto the market.
GM foods are potentially dangerous. Human health is at risk because, despite extensive testing, scientists cannot anticipate all the problems that might occur when food is modified. This risk will increase as biotechnology companies introduce more modifications. GM foods also present a danger to the environment. The use of these crops has resulted in fewer strains planted. If disease wipes out a few of these strains, the result could be catastrophic. In addition, removing certain varieties of crops wipes out the organisms that feed on them. Furthermore, pollen produced from GM crops can accidentally fertilize unmodified crops, polluting the natural gene pool. This cross-pollination, in turn, makes labeling foods impossible. Thus consumers will not be able to choose whether to purchase GM crops.	The fears about GM food are a result of media scares about "frankenfood." Few deaths have been directly attributed to genetic modification, and scientists are taking all reasonable precautions to ensure these products are safe. The need for many different strains is not an argument against GM crops. Scientists and farmers cannot produce and plant many different strains. Furthermore, scientists have no evidence that cross-pollination of GM with non GM varieties is harmful

(CONTINUES)

PROS	CONS
GM food will not help solve hunger in developing countries. The problem in such countries is not one of food production but of distribution (due to wars, for example), the emphasis on cash crops rather than staple crops (to pay off the national debt), and deforestation and desertification. In addition, many GM strains are infertile, forcing farmers to buy seed annually from companies that can charge whatever they want because they have a patent on the strain.	The possible benefits from GM food are enormous. Modifications that render plants less vulnerable to pests lead to less pesticide use, which is better for the environment. Other modifications increase crop yield, which leads to lower food prices. This technology is particularly important for developing countries; it can help farmers grow crops in arid soil. More important, it can help prevent diseases as the introduction of golden rice has shown.
Yes, banning GM food would decrease consumer choice. However, governments have the right and obligation to intervene to prevent harm to both the population and the environment. Besides, the number of consumers who actually want GM food is tiny.	Banning GM food would result in fewer choices for the consumer. Scientists can prevent cross-breeding between GM and non GM plants so that foods can be properly labeled and consumers can maintain their freedom of choice.

Source: The content on this page is taken from Editors of IDEA, *The Debatabase Book*, 3rd. ed. (New York: International Debate Education Association, 2007). Adapted from IDEA's on-line Debatabase at http://www.idebate.org.

Resource Sheet
Should Smoking Be Restricted?

Although most countries put age restrictions on the purchase of tobacco, over a billion adults smoke legally every day. Supplying this demand is big business. By the 1990s major tobacco companies had been forced to admit that their products were addictive and had serious health consequences, both for the user and for those subject to second-hand smoke. In the developed world, public opinion shifted against smoking. Many governments substantially increased taxes on tobacco to discourage smoking and to help pay for the costs of smoking-related illness. Yet, while smoking has declined among some groups, it has increased among the young. Meanwhile tobacco companies look to developing nations for new markets.

PROS	CONS
Smoking is extremely harmful to the smoker's health. The American Cancer Society estimates that tobacco causes up to 400,000 deaths each year—more than AIDS, alcohol, drug abuse, car crashes, murders, suicides, and fires combined. Worldwide some 3 million people die from smoking each year—one every 10 seconds. Estimates suggest that this figure will rise to 10 million by 2020. Smokers are 22 times more likely to develop lung cancer than nonsmokers, and smoking can lead to a host of other health problems, including emphysema and heart disease. One of the main responsibilities of any government is to ensure the safety of its population; that is why taking hard drugs and breaking the speed limit are illegal. Putting a ban on smoking would therefore be reasonable.	While a government has a responsibility to protect its population, it also has a responsibility to defend freedom of choice. The law prevents citizens from harming others. It should not stop people from behavior that threatens only themselves. Dangerous sports such as rock climbing and parachuting are legal. No laws have been passed against indulging in other health-threatening activities such as eating fatty foods or drinking too much alcohol. Banning smoking would be an unmerited intrusion into personal freedom.

(**Continues**)

PROS	CONS
Of course personal freedom is important—we should act against the tobacco companies, not individuals. If a company produces food that is poisonous or a car that fails safety tests, the product is immediately taken off the market. All cigarettes and other tobacco products are potentially lethal and should be taken off the market. In short, smoking should be banned.	Cigarettes are very different from dangerous cars or poisonous foods. Cigarettes are not dangerous because they are defective; they are only potentially harmful. People should still be permitted to smoke them. A better comparison is to unhealthy foods. Fatty foods can contribute to heart disease, obesity, and other conditions, but the government does not punish manufacturers of these products. Both cigarettes and fatty foods are sources of pleasure that, while having serious associated health risks, are only fatal after many decades. They are quite different from poisonous foods or unsafe cars, which pose high, immediate risks.
Smoking is not a choice, because nicotine is an addictive drug. Evidence suggests that tobacco companies deliberately produce the most addictive cigarettes they can. Up to 90% of smokers begin when they are under age 18, often due to peer pressure. Once addicted, continuing to smoke is no longer an issue of free choice but of chemical compulsion. The government should ban tobacco just as it does other addictive drugs like heroin and cocaine because it is the only way to force people to quit. Most smokers say that they want to kick the habit, so this legislation would be doing them a favor.	Comparing tobacco to hard drugs is inaccurate. Tobacco is not debilitating in the same way that many illegal narcotics are, it is not comparable to heroin in terms of addictiveness, and it is not a mind-altering substance that leads to irrational, violent, or criminal behavior. It is much less harmful than alcohol. Many other substances and activities can be addictive (e.g., coffee, physical exercise) but that is no reason to make them illegal. People are able to abstain—many give up smoking every year—if they choose to live a healthier life. Nevertheless, many enjoy smoking as part of their everyday life.
Most smokers are law-abiding citizens who would like to stop. They would not resort to criminal or black market activities if cigarettes were no longer legally available; they would just quit. Banning smoking would make them quit and massively lighten the burden on health resources.	Criminalizing an activity of about one-sixth of the world's population would be insane. As America's prohibition of alcohol during the 1920s showed, banning a popular recreational drug leads to crime. In addition, governments would lose the tax revenue from tobacco sales, which they could use to cover the costs of health care.

PROS	CONS
The effects of smoking are not restricted to smokers. Second-hand smoke jeopardizes the health of non-smokers as well. Research suggests that non-smoking partners of smokers have a greater chance of developing lung cancer than other non-smokers. Beyond the health risks, smoke can also be extremely unpleasant in the workplace or in bars and restaurants. Smoking causes discomfort as well as harm to others and should be banned.	The evidence that passive smoking causes health problems is very slim. At most, those who live with heavy smokers for a long time may have a very slightly increased risk of cancer. Smoke-filled environments can be unpleasant for non-smokers, but reasonable and responsible solutions can be found. Offices and airports could have designated smoking areas, and many restaurants offer patrons the choice of smoking and non-smoking sections. Allowing people to make their own decisions is surely always the best option. Restricting smoking in public places may sometimes be appropriate; banning it would be lunacy.
At the very least all tobacco advertising should be banned and cigarette packs should have even more prominent and graphic health warnings.	Where is the evidence that either of these measures would affect the rate of tobacco consumption? Cigarette companies claim that advertisements merely persuade people to switch brands, not start smoking. People start smoking because of peer pressure. Indeed, forbidding cigarettes will make them more attractive to adolescents. As for health warnings, if the knowledge that cigarettes have serious health risks deterred people from smoking, then no one would smoke. People start and continue to smoke in the full knowledge of the health risks.

Source: The content on this page is taken from Editors of IDEA, *The Debatabase Book*, 3rd. ed. (New York: International Debate Education Association, 2007). Adapted from IDEA's on-line Debatabase at http://www.idebate.org.

9. Open Forum

Instructional objectives

Students will be able to:

- formulate reasons in support of and in opposition to views and opinions on a number of issues
- interact with each other in a structured and systematic manner
- defend their position on certain issues and support and/or critique in a polite and constructive manner the opinions and views expressed by others
- think critically and build their responses under time pressure
- actively participate in full-class discussions
- actively connect new information to information previously learned
- use written sources of information to support their oral presentations
- analyze, synthesize, and infer from information
- apply self-monitoring and self-corrective strategies

Description

The class holds a group discussion during which students take turns presenting their own arguments and responding to arguments of others.

Time

45–60 minutes

Materials

Possible Open Forum Topics resource sheet (optional)

Guidelines for Open Forum Participants resource sheet (copy for each student)

Preparation

1. Choose a topic for the Open Forum—the more controversial the topic, the more ideas students will be able to generate in support and against the topic (see Possible Open Forum Topics for suggestions).

2. A week or two before the Forum, tell the students that they will be participating in a discussion of a topic of your choice. Announce the topic and ask the students to prepare for the Forum by listing arguments in support of and against the topic statement. Encourage the class to research the issue using a variety of sources in English: books, journals, Internet, etc., and to make notes. Students are to bring these notes to class on the day of the debate.

Class layout and grouping of students

Set the chairs in a circle so that the students can face each other during the lesson.

Procedure

1. On the day of the debate, organize the class in a circle or square. Distribute the Guidelines for Open Forum Participants and review. Explain to the students that during the Open Forum they are to express not only the views they agree with but also reasonable arguments and legitimate positions with which they disagree. They are to respond to as many different views as possible in order to keep the discussion going.

2. Stress the importance of listening and note taking during the exercise and encourage the students to refer to their notes during the Open Forum.

3. Begin the exercise by offering the first argument in support of or against the topic. Alternately, you can open the floor for discussion and invite a student to present his or her point.

4. Moderate the Open Forum by making sure that students present only one point at a time and that they abide by the guidelines. Make sure that all students participate.

5. If you think that the discussion may be dying out, introduce a controversial point.

6. Conclude the exercise by summarizing the main points and thank students for their participation.

Assessment

By observing students' interactions, you will see how well they can think on their feet and how quickly they can formulate their thoughts in English. You can also assess how well students have researched an issue and how well they have mastered relevant vocabulary.

Extensions and modifications

To make the forum more challenging, have the students toss a rolled-up sock or a softball to the next speaker. Make sure that the students do not pass the ball to the same person twice.

Possible Open Forum Topics

1. Debt Relief for Developing Countries
   http://www.idebate.org/debatabase/topic_details.php?topicID=424

2. Prohibition of School Prayer
   http://www.idebate.org/debatabase/topic_details.php?topicID=174

3. Censorship of the Arts
   http://www.idebate.org/debatabase/topic_details.php?topicID=17

4. Relaxation of Immigration Laws
   http://www.idebate.org/debatabase/topic_details.php?topicID=116

5. Lowering the Age of Consent
   http://www.idebate.org/debatabase/topic_details.php?topicID=299

6. Drugs for Athletes
   http://www.idebate.org/debatabase/topic_details.php?topicID=28

7. Gun control
   http://www.idebate.org/debatabase/topic_details.php?topicID=33

8. Should couples be banned from adopting children overseas?
   http://www.idebate.org/debatabase/topic_details.php?topicID=313

9. International Criminal Court
   http://www.idebate.org/debatabase/topic_details.php?topicID=146

10. Do animals have rights?
    http://www.idebate.org/debatabase/topic_details.php?topicID=8

For more ideas, topics, and other resources, go to http://www.idebate.org/debatabase/index.php.

Guidelines for Open Forum Participants

Each participant can choose one of the following options:

1. Present a new point on the topic (either for or against).
   For example: "I would like to introduce a new point into the Open Forum. My argument supports (opposes) the topic of today's discussion."

2. Respond critically to a point presented by another student. Please remember to summarize the point you are addressing before responding.
   For example: "I would like to disagree with my previous speaker(s) who argued that . . . My point is . . ."

3. Present support for another participant's argument. This support can be an example or evidence based on your research.
   For example: "I would like to further support the argument presented by . . ."

10. Corner Debates

Instructional objectives

Students will be able to:

- actively participate in small-group and full-class discussion
- actively connect new information to information previously learned
- work in teams to achieve common goals
- review and give feedback on the work of others
- observe, model, and critique how others speak and behave in a particular situation or setting

Description

Students will listen to a statement on a controversial topic and decide if they agree or disagree with the statement. After meeting with students on the opposing team and discussing their reasons why, they will be asked the question again and reassigned to a position team if necessary. They will then each have to take part in a debate in which they defend the position opposite to their belief.

Time

60 minutes

Materials

Four large posters or flip chart sheets each labeled with one of the following: Strongly Disagree, Disagree, Strongly Agree, Agree

A short list of controversial topics such as

- America was right to invade Iraq.
- The government should place sin taxes on non-essential items like cigarettes, alcohol, and snack/junk food.

Slip of paper for each student

Pens

Stopwatch or clock with second hand

Class layout and grouping of students

Clear the four corners of your classroom to create an area big enough for a group of students to sit and discuss their viewpoints. One option is to shove all the desks to the middle of the room when you are about to begin.

Procedure

Part I: Preparation

1. Tell the students that they are about to hear a statement that may be controversial. Distribute a slip of paper to each student. When you read the statement aloud, tell them that they are not to speak just yet, but rather they will first be asked to voice their opinion by walking to the poster that best mirrors their opinion. Point out the four posters in the corners and tell everyone to stand and push their desks into the middle of the room so that they can begin the activity.

2. Read the statement aloud. Give the students no more than five minutes to decide if they strongly agree, agree, strongly disagree, or disagree with the statement you just gave. Tell them to write their decision on the paper and walk to the corner that corresponds to their opinion. If you have a disproportionately high number of students on one side of the issue, simply send everyone back to the center of the room and read another statement that will yield more balanced groups.

3. Once all students have assembled into their groups, assign one member of each group to be the Opinion Coordinator. The Opinion Coordinator ensures that all students in the group get a chance to speak.

4. Give the groups 5–10 minutes to discuss the reasons for their opinion and to develop a list of at least 5 for their stand.

5. As they discuss, prepare the next step, in which you will pair students with students on opposing sides of the statement. This will vary depending on the numbers of students in each group, but basically you should aim to pair students from the groups of Strongly Agree with Strongly Disagree, and Agree with Disagree.

6. Tell the students that are about to be paired up with a student from an opposing group—Strongly Agree with Strongly Disagree, Agree with Disagree—and they should keep their paper visible to ensure they are paired appropriately. Explain to the students that they should find a student on the opposing side to pair up with and taking any 2 desks from the middle of the room, place the desks together.

7. They will now have 10 minutes to share their differing opinions. Both students in the pairs must have the chance to share at least 3 of the reasons why they believe as they do. After 10 minutes, informally assess if the groups need more time, and if necessary, give the groups no more than 2 extra minutes to wrap up their discussions.

8. After 10 minutes, tell the students to once again move the desks to the center of the room. Tell them that you will repeat the original statement. The students will once again have the opportunity to vote by going to the corner that corresponds to their opinion. They may change their decision from their original choice if they now feel differently. Repeat the statement and have the students go to the corner of the room that best reflects their opinion.

9. Poll the students and see if anyone has changed her opinion based on her discussions either within their team or with a student from the opposing team. If so, discuss briefly what caused those students to change their minds—was it the persistence of the people they were arguing against?

Part II: Debate

1. Ask three of the students who changed their decision from the first poll to the second to serve as judges. Choose one student to serve as chair and then chose two students from each of the two teams of Strongly Agree and Strongly Disagree to debate the statement. The remainder of the class will serve as the audience and help the judges to make a decision at the end of the debate.

2. Now explain that debating has nothing to do with how one personally feels about an issue and that while it is always easier to have a personal opinion that agrees with the side you are defending, a debater doesn't need to agree with his or her side in order to win a debate. In light of this, explain that the two teams will now have to present and defend the opinion or side in the debate that is opposite to the one that they personally hold.

3. Explain that they will now give and hear two different kinds of speeches—constructive and rebuttal speeches. The constructive speech given by each team outlines the team's argument. The rebuttal speech given by each team addresses points made against their argument by the opposing team as well as tries to convince the judges that their argument is the stronger one by highlighting inconsistencies in the other team's arguments. Explain that they now have five minutes to prepare their constructive and rebuttal speeches for the following debate format.

1st Affirmative Constructive	5 minutes
1st Negative Constructive	5 minutes
2nd Affirmative Rebuttal	4 minutes
2nd Negative Rebuttal	4 minutes

4. As the two teams prepare, have the audience arrange the room into a debating layout with two debaters per side, an area for three judges at the back of the room, and a chair at the front. After five minutes, have the debaters, judge, and chair take their places.

5. Instruct the chair to begin and keep time for each speech. Judges should take notes on the arguments that are made and ensure that rebuttals address points made by the opposing team.

6. After the debate concludes, quickly convene the judges and privately ask for their decision on who won the debate. Turn to the audience and say that you will now ask them for their opinion on who won by a show of hands. Say, "Affirmative. Who feels affirmative should win?" Count the hands and then say, "Negative. Who feels negative should win?" Compare and see which team won according to the audience. Now ask the judges to share their decision. If you agree, say so and explain why you think so. If you don't agree, explain why you feel the other team should be declared the winner.

7. Ask the debaters how they felt about arguing for the side whose view they opposed. At some point did they start to believe what they were saying in order to be convincing? Has their opinion changed? If not, are they more sympathetic to the other side's point of view? Have they learned any new insights into the issue from this exercise?

8. You may choose to hold a vote with the four corners one more time and see how the numbers have changed throughout the lesson.

Assessment

There are many opportunities for informal assessment. Walk the room and listen for student-to-student responses and questions and assess understanding of the objectives.

11. Debate Auditions

Description

Students "audition" for a place in the Big Debate through elimination rounds of various debate speeches. The Big Debate will take place between the winning speakers from the previous day's auditions.

Time

3 class periods of 45–60 minutes each

Materials

Debate Format resource sheet (copy for each student)

Preparation

Choose a debate topic of interest to your students. (See http://www.idebate.org/debatabase/index.php for a list of over 100 possible topics.)

Class layout and grouping of students

Students receive their initial directions in their regular seating arrangement. For the debate, set the classroom as an auditorium with desks and chairs for the debaters and a chair facing the audience.

Procedure

Day 1—Research

No more than one to two days before you plan to hold a team debate, facilitate a discussion on the value of debate for a democratic society. Explain to the students that they will participate in a debate on a topic you have selected.

1. Distribute copies of the Debate Format resource sheet and discuss. Address any questions that the students may have.

2. Explain that although only a select number of students will be able to debate at one time, all students will eventually debate. Organize the students into pairs and tell them to prepare both sides of the topic. They are to brainstorm different ideas on the topic and research evidence and support for their arguments. Encourage the students to use a variety of sources in English: books, journals, the Internet, etc. Tell them that they can bring their notes to the debate. Encourage students to prepare as teams and support each other in their preparation.

Day 2—The Debate

1. Explain that everyone is about to take part in a debate and students will be able to analyze and critique their own as well as others' debate speeches. Explain that the class will hold a Big Debate during the next class session. All students will have the opportunity to be team members of the Big Debate, but they must first take part in debate auditions.

2. Tell the class that they will audition for each of the six speeches in the Big Debate. Divide the class into six groups: potential 1st Affirmative Constructive Speaker; potential 1st Negative Constructive Speaker; and so on. The members of each group will deliver the speech assigned the group while the rest of the class listens and takes notes. Once all members of the group have finished speaking, the audience will be asked to critique and analyze the speeches and determine who did the best job of presenting that particular speech. The student who is chosen as having given the best speech in his or her group, based on points made, counterarguments addressed, etc., will go on to the Big Debate. (Also choose a runner-up in case the winner is not in class the day of the debate.) The students who are not chosen become members of the audience. Once the best speaker/ speech is chosen for the Affirmative Constructive, continue the process for the other speeches. It is important that students keep notes throughout to ensure that the points presented in the first speeches correlate with those in the later speeches. This is a test for both the speakers and the audience.

3. In order to help students remember the various roles of each speech and speaker, review the Debate Format resource sheet, emphasizing the various roles and time restrictions for each speech. Ensure that everyone understands the procedure.

4. Introduce the topic statement and ask the members of the 1st Affirmative Constructive group to come to the front of the room and present their speeches. The audience should choose a winner and be able to give a rationale for their choice. Continue until the class has chosen a winner for all speeches.

5. Explain that for the Big Debate to take place, you need a chair and one to three judges (depending on the size of your class). Select one student as the chair and one to three students to be judges.

Day 3—The Big Debate

1. The winners of each debate speech from the previous day will present a cohesive speech on the topic. You may use this opportunity to analyze strategies, construction of all speeches, etc. or you may choose to simply showcase the smooth flow of a speech.

2. Allow 10 minutes of preparation time for the debaters. As they prepare, explain to the rest of the class the role of the chair. Explain that the chair is to moderate the debate, keep time, and keep the debaters to the format and timing. Explain that the role of the judges is to track the arguments of each team as well as rebuttals made by each team. In tracking these arguments, they must ensure that teams are responding to counterpoints or attacks on their position made by the other team, while also appropriately attacking the other team's points. Whoever does a better job of answering all the opposing team's points and rebuttals and convincing the judges that their position is best defended should be the winner. Refer to the Judging Sheet (page xx) and ask if there are any questions. If you have not previously used the Judging Sheet with this classroom, explain the process to complete the sheet.

3. When the students are ready, prepare the classroom for the debate by setting up desks for the debaters and a chair, picking one to three judges, and assigning the remaining students as the audience.

4. When everyone is ready, begin the debate. Monitor the progress of the debate and take notes for the debriefing and feedback.

5. Conclude the debate by thanking the participants and audience and congratulating the speakers on their performance.

6. Discuss with the entire class the debate speeches they saw given yesterday and the entire debate they watched today. What differences did they see in the two? Did the debate auditions yesterday help them to understand what differentiates a good debate speech from a bad one?

Assessment

By observing how the students assess each other on their speeches and ultimately decide a winner, you can see how well students understand the basics of a good speech and the necessary points to include in a specific debate speech. You may choose to use a rubric that is tailored to the topic statement to be debated (see Chapter 5).

Extensions and Modifications

Distribute the Judging Sheet to all members of the audience to give them practice judging. It would also be good to have debaters get additional feedback and for judges to compare their assessments of the debate with the audience. In this instance the teacher is the ultimate decision maker on who wins.

Debate Format

Participants: two teams of three speakers

Format:

1st Affirmative Speaker (A1)	constructive speech	5 minutes
1st Negative Speaker (N1)	constructive speech	5 minutes
2nd Affirmative Speaker (A2)	rebuttal speech	4 minutes
2nd Negative Speaker (N2)	rebuttal speech	4 minutes
3rd Affirmative Speaker (A3)	summation speech	4 minutes
3rd Negative Speaker (N3)	summation speech	4 minutes

Preparation time (only for the Big Debate):
Each team has a total of six minutes preparation time.

Roles of individual speakers:

First Affirmative Speaker (A1): presents the affirmative's case, which includes the team's understanding and interpretation of the topic and its arguments supporting the topic (usually not more than four).

First Negative Speaker (N1): presents the negative's case, which includes the team's understanding and interpretation of the topic and its arguments supporting the topic (usually not more than four). Responds to (refutes) the affirmative's case.

Second Affirmative Speaker (A2): extends the First Affirmative's arguments by providing additional reasoning and evidence. A2 rebuilds (rebuts) affirmative arguments that N1 attacked and refutes the First Negative's arguments.

Second Negative Speaker (N2): extends the N1's arguments by providing additional reasoning and evidence. N2 also rebuilds (rebuts) negative arguments that A2 attacked and refutes arguments presented by A1 and A2 in their constructive and rebuttal speeches.

Third Affirmative Speaker (A3): summarizes the affirmative's arguments, emphasizing the most important elements, and attempts to demonstrate why the affirmative team should win the debate.

Third Negative Speaker (N3): summarizes the negative's arguments, emphasizing the most important elements, and attempts to demonstrate why the negative should win the debate.

12. Flow of a Debate

Instructional objectives

Students will be able to:

- formulate reasons in support of and in opposition to views and opinions on a number of issues in a written form

- defend their position on certain issues and support and/or critique in a polite and constructive manner the opinions and views expressed by others

- think critically and build their responses under time pressure

- appropriately structure their written presentations to fit the assigned word limits

- communicate in teams and assist each other in order to achieve common goals

- understand and select relevant information from the text

Description

This lesson uses a written debate to introduce students to the process of flowing debate.

Time

45–60 minutes

Materials

Flip-chart paper and pens (for each group)

Model Debate Flow resource sheet (copy for each student)

Preparation

Choose an appropriate topic for a debate. Make sure that it allows students on both sides to present reasonable arguments. (See http://www.idebate.org/debatabase/index.php for a list of over 100 possible topics.)

Class layout and grouping of students

Arrange the classroom so that students can work in groups of three to five.

Procedure

1. Explain to the students that they will participate in a debate on a topic of your choice, but instead of presenting their arguments orally as individuals, they will work as a team and write their arguments on a sheet of flip-chart paper. Distribute copies of the Model Debate Flow sheet for review and highlight how a flow typically looks after a debate has concluded. Divide the class into four teams of three to five students. If you have a larger class, simply create more teams of three to five students. Note that if you create more than four groups, have the teams write each student's initials in the upper right corner of the flip chart paper for easy retrieval later in the exercise. Distribute flip-chart paper and pens to each team and ask them to divide the paper vertically into four even columns. Once they have divided the page, label the columns as follows:

First Affirmative	First Negative	Second Affirmative	Second Negative

2. Tell the students that they have five minutes to write down no more than four arguments in support of the topic in the first column on the left. They should number the items and present them in the order of importance, just as points are delivered in a debate. This mimics the first affirmative's presentation in a debate. Stress that they must present their arguments clearly and concisely so that other teams can understand their opinions.

3. After five minutes, call, "SWITCH," and ask the groups to pass their flip-chart paper to the team on their right.

4. Give the groups seven minutes to read what the other team presented and counter each argument. Tell the teams to write their arguments clearly and concisely in the second column. Point out that this mimics how the first negative speaker would respond to the affirmative's case in a debate.

5. After seven minutes, call, "SWITCH" and ask the groups to pass their flip-chart paper to the team on their right. Give them nine minutes to read the arguments and respond. This response mimics that of the second affirmative speaker.

6. After nine minutes, call, "SWITCH" and ask the groups to pass their flip-chart paper to the team on their right. Give them eleven minutes to read the arguments and respond. This response mimics that of the second negative speaker.

7. After eleven minutes, call, "SWITCH" and, again, pass their flip-chart paper to the team on their right, which should be the team that started the completed chart. If you formed more than four groups for this exercise, have the teams now return the sheet to the team in their group that started that particular chart paper.

8. Conclude the exercise by asking the groups to read each column and see which arguments were addressed, which were forgotten, and who they think may win the argument based on this flow sheet. Tell the affirmative that although they were the first to present their case, they must judge the evidence presented with an objective mind.

Assessment

1. By observing interactions between students, you will be able to assess how well students can think on their feet and how quickly they can formulate their thoughts in English.

2. You will be able to assess the quality of students' written work by collecting the flip-chart papers after the exercise (it may be a good idea to give each team a different color marker to make it easier for you to identify their responses).

Extensions and modifications

You can ask your students to write an argumentative essay on the debate topic.

Model Debate Flow

1st TEAM (affirmative)	2nd TEAM (negative)	3rd TEAM (affirmative)	4th TEAM (negative)
1st ARGUMENT	1st RESPONSE	1st RESPONSE	1st RESPONSE
2nd ARGUMENT	2nd RESPONSE	2nd RESPONSE	2nd RESPONSE
3rd ARGUMENT	3rd RESPONSE	3rd RESPONSE	3rd RESPONSE
4th ARGUMENT	4th RESPONSE	4th RESPONSE	4th RESPONSE
	1st NEW ARGUMENT	RESPONSE to 1st ARGUMENT	1st RESPONSE
	2nd NEW ARGUMENT	RESPONSE to 2nd ARGUMENT	2nd RESPONSE
	3rd NEW ARGUMENT	RESPONSE to 3rd ARGUMENT	3rd RESPONSE

Chapter 4
Introduction to Role Plays and Simulations

Role plays and simulations promote critical thinking and creativity, encourage students to take risks with new language, and help develop cooperative skills in a safe setting. These exercises also compel students to think on their feet. Unlike skits or plays, role plays do not have scripts. Rather, students are assigned roles and given a scenario with different elements and complications that they must address in their roles. For example, students may role-play tourists and tour guides who must deal with a flooded town or a situation in which all hotels are booked.

The activities in this section involve role playing and simulations to teach ESL.

13. Getting to Know You

Instructional objectives

Students will be able to:

- demonstrate good comprehension during a variety of conversations by verbally and non-verbally responding appropriately

- negotiate and manage interaction with other learners to accomplish tasks

- use written sources of information to support their oral presentations

- paraphrase, summarize, elaborate, clarify, ask relevant questions, and make relevant comments in conversation, debate, and simulations

- negotiate and initiate conversations by questioning, restating, soliciting information, and paraphrasing the communication of others

Students also will practice multi-processing, speaking and listening to new information about other people in fast-paced conversation.

Description

The lesson helps students develop the social skills they need when meeting someone for the first time and emphasizes the importance of getting to know that individual and remembering what they have learned about him or her.

Time

45–60 minutes

Materials

Role-Play Identity activity sheet (copy for each student)

Getting to Know You resource sheet (copy for each student)

Remember Me? activity sheet (copy for each student)

Class layout and grouping of students

Students remain in their seats to receive directions and to fill out their role-play sheets. They then circulate to introduce themselves to the other "attendees" and fill out the work sheet. They return to their desks after they have completed the work sheet.

Procedure

1. Explain to the students that they will be simulating a situation in which they are attending a debate conference for the first time. They are expected to be friendly and to find out more about the other "debaters." Point out that courtesy demands that they listen carefully so they can remember what each debater said. Tell them that they will be quizzed about how much they remember.

2. Distribute Role-Play Identity activity sheet and tell the students that they are to use the sheet to create an "identity" for one of the attendees. Review the sheet and ask the students to fill it out. (If you are planning to use the extension activity, ask them to write their name on the back of the sheet.)

3. Collect the sheets and distribute them randomly. Tell the students to read and memorize the identity information on their sheet so they can portray that person accurately.

4. Distribute Getting to Know You resource sheet. Discuss the sheet and present each phrase in a mock conversation to demonstrate how and when it is used.

5. Tell the students that the classroom is now the conference center where the debaters have gathered prior to the day's sessions. They are to mingle and meet as many people as possible in 15–30 minutes (depending on the number of students present). Remind the students that they must assume the identity of the person on their role-play sheet and gather as much information about the other debaters as possible. They can use the phrases you have introduced to begin their conversations. If a debater asks them a question whose answer is not on their role-play sheet, they should make one up—but always remain in character. As the students mingle, make sure they are using appropriate conversation starters and etiquette.

6. After time is up, call, "TIME!" Distribute the Remember Me? activity sheet and review the rules. Tell the students that they have five minutes to fill in the chart on the activity sheet. After five minutes, call time and ask the students to return to their desks.

7. Review the charts briefly to see who has the most signatures.

8. Have the students turn in their Role-Play Identity sheets. Read each character description without the name and see if the students can guess the name of the debater you have described.

Assessment

You can assess performance as the students circulate, introducing themselves to and carrying on conversations with other debaters. Correct when necessary.

Extensions and Modifications

Have each student keep circulating until she finds the person who is holding the Role-Play Identity sheet that she wrote.

Role-Play Identity

Name (make one up): _____.

School I Am Attending (check one):

_____ Jones International, Honolulu

_____ King High School, Detroit

_____ #53 Government School, Prague (Czech Republic)

_____ The Learning Academy, Budapest (Hungary)

_____ Royal School of Arts, Plymouth (United Kingdom)

Interests (choose three):

_____ Being with family

_____ Dating

_____ Debating

_____ Driving

_____ Eating

_____ Football

_____ Playing computer games

_____ Reading

_____ Scuba diving

_____ Sewing

_____ Shopping

_____ Skating

_____ Skiing

_____ Sleeping

_____ Traveling

_____ Water polo

_____ Writing

Unique Trait (Create your own. You may have up to three for this activity.):

- _____

- _____

- _____

Getting to Know You

- Nice to meet you.

- Pleasure to meet you.

- I have heard a lot about you.

- How are you doing?

- Great day for debating—what do you think?

- Did you find your way here okay?

- What's new in Budapest/Honolulu/Detroit/Prague/Plymouth?

- I was in Budapest/Honolulu/Detroit/Prague/Plymouth three years ago for a conference. Do they still have that great blues club/nature museum/visitors' bureau/gay pride parade?

- How long have you lived there?

- What brings you all the way here?

- Know where I can find a great blues club/CD store/comic shop?

- I'd like you to meet my new friend, X.

- X, this is Y. Y, this is X.

- So, what do you like to do in your spare time?

Remember Me?

Instructions: Fill in the chart below by asking each of the debaters you have just met one of the questions. If the debater answers yes, he or she signs the appropriate box (using his or her debater name). For example, a student may ask Alice Springs if she likes to sew. If she says yes, then she signs that box. (The "free fact" boxes are for other information students may have picked up in their conversations.) After the debater signs a box OR if she says no, you must move on to a new person with a new question. You may return to a debater later but may not ask him or her two consecutive questions. Your goal is to fill in as many squares as possible in five minutes.

Likes to scuba dive?	Lives in Prague?	Attends Royal School of Arts?	Likes to sew?	Free fact
___	___	___	___	___
Attends #53 Government School?	Free fact	Likes to play on the computer?	Attends Jones International?	Attends The Learning Academy?
___	___	___	___	___
Likes to be with family?	Likes to travel?	Lives in Detroit?	Likes to debate?	Likes to sleep?
___	___	___	___	___
Free fact	Lives in Honolulu?	Likes to play football?	Free fact	Likes to drive?
___	___	___	___	___
Lives in Hungary?	Likes to read?	Likes to ski?	Likes to play water polo?	Lives in Plymouth?
___	___	___	___	___

14. What Am I?

Instructional objectives

Students will be able to:

- use responsive listening
- paraphrase, summarize, elaborate, clarify, ask relevant questions, and make relevant comments in conversation, debate, and simulations
- negotiate and initiate conversations by questioning, restating, soliciting information, and paraphrasing the communication of others
- appropriately seek support and feedback from others
- analyze, synthesize, and infer from information
- use vocabulary to describe and ask about abstract concepts
- multi-process listening and speaking skills

Description

The teacher tapes a concept word to the back of each student. The students must then circulate to find out what word they are.

Time

45 minutes

Materials

Government and Emotion Concepts resource sheet

small pieces of paper

tape or pins

Assorted Concept Tags resource sheet (optional)

Preparation

Create one tag for each student, using the terms on Government and Emotion Concepts.

Class layout and grouping of students

The students receive their tags at their desks and then walk around the classroom during the exercise.

Procedure

1. Define and discuss the meaning of abstract concept.

    Definition: An abstract concept is a term or thought that refers to a quality, an emotion, or an idea such as "sensitivity" or "imperialism," rather than to a solid or concrete object such as a "truck" or a "football." Discuss abstract concepts with the students as appropriate or needed.

2. Explain to the students that you will tape an abstract concept involving politics or states of mind to their back. Discuss types of politics or governments and states of mind you will be using so the students can narrow down the universe of words. You may also choose to make a transparency of the resource sheet to give students a preview of the words that will be used in the exercise.

3. Tell the students that they are to ask enough yes or no, or yes AND no questions of another student to guess the concept. As an example, explain that you might have the word sensitivity on your back. To guess your word, you might ask the following questions:

a.	Is it a type of government?	NO
b.	Is it an emotion?	YES
c.	Is it a concept related to business?	NO
d.	Is it a feeling or emotion?	YES and NO
e.	Is it something you learned about in school?	YES

    The questioning should continue until each student guesses the name of his or her concept. Once they guess, they should circulate to help others students guess their concept.

Assessment

You can informally assess the students' quality of questions.

Extensions and modifications

Once the students have all guessed their tags, have them repeat the exercise using either the words on Assorted Concept Tags resource sheet or words they have chosen.

Government and Emotion Concepts

Marxism

Anarchy

Aristocracy

Theocracy

Dictatorship

Democracy

Monarchy

Socialist state

Confederacy

Federal republic

Totalitarian state

Oligarchy

Happiness

Anger

Love Hate

Fear

Peace

Joy

Sorrow

Reverence

Guilt

Hope

Jealousy

Remorse

Sadness

Surprise

Disgust

Boredom

Anticipation

Assorted Concept Tags

Third World debt

Poverty

Colonization

Globalization

Human rights

Procrastination

War

Knowledge

Power

Design

Format

Confusion

Spirituality

Representation

Methodology

Objective

Answer

Desire

Emotion

Dream

Charisma

Invisibility

Ambitions

Unity

Pride

15. You Oughta Be in Pictures

Instructional objectives

Students will be able to:

- demonstrate good comprehension during a variety of conversations by verbally and non-verbally responding appropriately
- follow oral and written directions
- negotiate and manage interaction with other learners to accomplish tasks
- initiate and sustain conversations about a range of topics
- elaborate and extend other people's ideas and words
- persuade, argue, negotiate, evaluate, and justify in a variety of contexts
- show awareness of and exhibit sensitivity to gender and cultural bias issues and concerns
- use culturally and socially appropriate non-verbal communication in social and formal interactions
- use acceptable tone, volume, stress, and intonation, in various settings and with various audiences

Description

Students audition for a role in a movie in which the scenes keep changing.

Time

45–60 minutes

Materials

sheet of paper (for each student)

marker (for each group)

pins (for each student)

Sample Scenes resource sheet

Preparation

Print out the Sample Scenes sheet and cut into strips.

Class layout and grouping of students

Students work in groups of four.

Procedure

1. Tell the students that you are the casting director who has come to audition actors for a new movie. You will choose the actors based on their performance of a scene from the film. However, although you know what the scene is about, you don't have a script, so they will have to act impromptu. Explain that you get bored easily and so you will likely change the scene, the roles, and the actors every so often.

2. Organize the students in groups of four. Ask the students in each group to count off from one to four so that each person has a number. Distribute the paper, markers, and pins. Tell the students to write their number on the paper—large enough so that everyone can see it—and pin it on.

3. Explain the exercise:

   a. You will ask one of the groups to come to the front of the room and assign them a setting and roles. When you say, "START," you will point to an actor who begins the scene anyway that he or she wishes. The other actors should jump in whenever they have something to add. Remind the actors to keep the other roles in mind and so they should say something that will help the others contribute to the scene.

   b. Periodically, you will say, "SWITCH ACTORS!" or "SWITCH SCENES!"

   c. If you say "SWITCH ACTORS!" the actors currently "on stage" must sit, and you choose a new group to take over the scene. Actors who have not yet contributed to the scene cannot sit down but must take part in the new scene in a new role. The teacher should start the new scene by pointing to an actor who hasn't contributed and calling out a new role that fits the scene. He may be seated only after the scene finishes and he has participated.

   d. If you say, "SWITCH SCENES!" the group stays on stage but begins a new scene.

4. After you have explained the procedure, ask one group to come to the front of the room to help you demonstrate, using the following scene. Then begin the exercise using the suggestions on the Scenes resource sheet or those you have developed.

Scene: Santa's Workshop in the North Pole

   Actor 1: A disgruntled elf who hates cold weather

   Actor 2: Mrs. Claus

   Actor 3: Rudolf the Reindeer's girlfriend

   Actor 4: A union representative

Extensions and modifications

Have the students create their own scenes or contribute a character to a scene.

Sample Scenes

Scene: A Café in Paris

Actor 1: A waiter in a café

Actor 2: A young American girl who recently arrived in Paris and is looking for love

Actor 3: A young poor French man who is looking for adventure

Actor 4: A Japanese tourist who lost her wallet

Scene: The Statue of Liberty, New York City

Actor 1: A tourist from Namibia who pretends to have an American accent

Actor 2: A professional clown who is looking for work

Actor 3: A police officer who didn't get enough sleep last night

Actor 4: A future president of the United States

Scene: On a Beach in the South Pacific

Actor 1: A lifeguard with amnesia

Actor 2: A famous Hollywood actor who just had plastic surgery and is trying to hide his face

Actor 3: The Dalai Lama

Actor 4: An Olympic athlete who just lost the medal she always carries with her

Scene: The Pyramids of Giza in Egypt

Actor 1: A scientist who just discovered the cure for cancer

Actor 2: A photographer visiting Paris from Italy

Actor 3: Santa Claus

Actor 4: A teacher with a class of 32 students

Scene: A Water Park in Canada

Actor 1: A student on spring break

Actor 2: An international spy looking for a diamonds dealer

Actor 3: A mother of three—with a past

Actor 4: The Pope

Scene: An Office Supply Store in Bulgaria

Actor 1: A high school student with 17 siblings

Actor 2: A dairy farmer from Iowa

Actor 3: A famous author on a book tour

Actor 4: Talk show host Larry King

Scene: The Floating Market in Thailand

Actor 1: A speedboat salesman

Actor 2: Oprah Winfrey

Actor 3: A baby who cannot speak but is hungry

Actor 4: A seamstress on vacation

Scene: A Restaurant in Jakarta, Indonesia

Actor 1: UN Secretary General Ban Ki-moon

Actor 2: A waitress who wants to become an actress

Actor 3: A dictator of a Marxist country in Africa

Actor 4: A nun

Scene: The Great Barrier Reef, Australia

Actor 1: A scuba diving instructor who just was released from prison

Actor 2: A director of Bollywood movies

Actor 3: German Chancellor Angela Merkel on a vacation

Actor 4: A dancer from the 1950s

Scene: School Board Meeting in Bolivia

Actor 1: Indigenous leader who just became president

Actor 2: Small child whose mother can't afford to send her to school

Actor 3: Animal rights activist

Actor 4: The Queen of England

16. Cultural Lessons

Instructional objectives

Students will be able to:

- select and utilize different resources to help understand language
- negotiate and manage interaction with other learners to accomplish tasks
- recognize the need for help and seek assistance appropriately from others
- interpret and respond appropriately to non-verbal cues and body language
- use written sources of information to support their oral presentations
- analyze, synthesize, and infer from information
- analyze the social context to determine appropriate language use
- show awareness of and exhibit sensitivity to gender and cultural bias issues and concerns
- use culturally and socially appropriate non-verbal communication in social and formal interactions
- observe, model, and critique how others speak and behave in a particular situation or setting

Description

This simulation involves learning how to read body language, gestures, and nonverbal language in different cultures.

Time

45–60 minutes

Materials

Briefing Sheet for the British Cultural Advisors (copy for each advisor)

Briefing Sheet for the Chicagawan Nationals (copy for each national)

Briefing Sheet for the British Expatriates (copy for each expatriate)

Briefing Sheet for the New British Ambassador

Name tags or small pieces of paper

pins or tape

Preparation

Cut the Briefing Sheet for the British Cultural Advisors along the dotted lines so that you have 10 separate slips of paper. Note: each paragraph is slightly different. Do not alert the students that they have received different slips.

Class layout and grouping of students

Students will receive their directions in their regular seating arrangement and then meet in groups around the room. For the ambassador's address, arrange the desks so that the ambassador faces the Chicagawan nationals and British expatriates while the British advisors face the audience from the side.

Procedure

1. Tell the students that they are about to take part in a simulation to help them understand how social and cultural norms differ. Explain that cultural and social norms are the behaviors, language, gestures, and body language that are used to communicate within a culture.

2. Tell the students that this exercise will simulate what can happen if we don't understand different cultures. You will assign roles to everyone in the class to carry out this simulation. The different roles are

   - The British ambassador to Chicagawa
   - The noted Chicagawan nationals
   - 10 British cultural advisors to the ambassador
   - British expatriates

   The setting is the British embassy in Chicagawa, a country with complex cultural norms that are often different from those of the British. The new British ambassador is about to make a speech at a reception for noted Chicagawan guests and many British expatriates.

3. Select a flexible, outgoing student to be the ambassador. He or she could make or break this lesson, so choose wisely. Then assign the other roles. Have the students wear small tags indicating their role to prevent any confusion during the exercise.

4. Distribute the instruction sheets for each role and give the students 10 minutes to read and prepare. Tell them that they may gather with other members of their group, but they may not share their instructions with other groups.

5. Circulate to make sure that the students understand their roles. Remind the Chicagawan nationals that they are to be obvious about showing their displeasure with any cultural faux pas. They can frown, walk away, glare, and so forth. If the ambassador corrects his or her mistake, they should smile and continue to listen politely until he or she makes another mistake.

6. After 10 minutes, ask the students to arrange the room for the speech and reception. Once the room is ready, tell the ambassador to begin. Feel free to call a Time Out if there is any confusion or if students are not playing their roles appropriately.

7. Once the ambassador has finished speaking, ask the British and Chicagawa to mingle. They should try to talk to at least three different people and find something new about each one—it can even be a small thing such as the person's name. Circulate to watch the interaction.

8. After 10–20 minutes, ask the students to return their desks to their original positions and sit down for a discussion.

9. Using the following questions, hold a Socratic discussion on how the speech and reception went. Have the students who played British expatriates help lead the discussion, but allow representatives from all the roles to speak.

   - What was the hardest thing about this exercise?
   - Who had the most difficult role in this exercise?
   - How did the ambassador do? Back up your comments with examples of behaviors observed during the exercise.
   - What was the role of the British expatriates?

10. Invite a representative from each of the three groups to stand and read their instruction sheet aloud. Then invite comments and questions. Continue until all groups have read. You may use the following questions to guide the discussion:

    - How are the instructions different?
    - Why did different groups receive different instructions?
    - What was the purpose of this?
    - Did it affect the outcome of the speech and reception? How?

11. Finally, ask the expatriates to share their analysis of how they think the Chicagawan nationals received the ambassador, the advisors, and the British expatriates themselves.

Assessment

By observing interactions and seeing how well the students correct their behavior based on non-verbal feedback, you will see how well students think on their feet. This is an excellent exercise to observe how quickly students respond to negative feedback in conversation and speeches.

Briefing Sheet for the British Cultural Advisors

The Chicagawa are a proud people who value respect from foreigners highly. Failure to show respect is a very serious insult, and they do not forgive easily. You are one of the cultural advisors to the new British ambassador to Chicagawa, a country that has just become important for Britain because of newly found oil reserves. You have been in Chicagawa only a short time, but you must help the ambassador prepare for his first reception with important Chicagawans. He is running late, and you and the other advisors have only 10 minutes to help him prepare. Good luck!

The Chicagawan people have a very established code of respect related to body language, gestures, and speech, including

- Stick out your tongue when greeting.

The Chicagawa are a proud people who value respect from foreigners highly. Failure to show respect is a very serious insult, and they do not forgive easily. You are one of the cultural advisors to the new British ambassador to Chicagawa, a country that has just become important for Britain because of newly found oil reserves. You have been in Chicagawa only a short time, but you must help the ambassador prepare for his first reception with important Chicagawans. He is running late, and you and the other advisors have only 10 minutes to help him prepare. Good luck!

The Chicagawan people have an established code of respect related to body language, gestures, and speech, including

- On greeting, shake their right pinky with your index finger ONLY for two shakes.

The Chicagawa are a proud people who value respect from foreigners highly. Failure to show respect is a very serious insult, and they do not forgive easily. You are one of the cultural advisors to the new British ambassador to Chicagawa, a country that has just become important for Britain because of newly found oil reserves. You have been in Chicagawa only a short time, but you must help the ambassador prepare for his first reception with important Chicagawans. He is running late, and you and the other advisors have only 10 minutes to help him prepare. Good luck!

The Chicagawan people have an established code of respect related to body language, gestures, and speech, including

- When speaking, only look at the women. They are the heads of the households and should be respected as such.

The Chicagawa are a proud people who value respect from foreigners highly. Failure to show respect is a very serious insult, and they do not forgive easily. You are one of the cultural advisors to the new British ambassador to Chicagawa, a country that has just become important for Britain because of newly found oil reserves. You have been in Chicagawa only a short time, but you must help the ambassador prepare for his first reception with important Chicagawans. He is running late, and you and the other advisors have only 10 minutes to help him prepare. Good luck!

The Chicagawan people have an established code of respect related to body language, gestures, and speech, including

- When speaking to a man, remember to refer to him by his wife's last name. For example, if you are meeting Serebe Falusi and his wife, Tebere Hansa, refer to the man as Serebe, Serebe Falusi, or Mr. Hansa, but NEVER as Mr. Falusi.

The Chicagawa are a proud people who value respect from foreigners highly. Failure to show respect is a very serious insult, and they do not forgive easily. You are one of the cultural advisors to the new British ambassador to Chicagawa, a country that has just become important for Britain because of newly found oil reserves. You have been in Chicagawa only a short time, but you must help the ambassador prepare for his first reception with important Chicagawans. He is running late, and you and the other advisors have only 10 minutes to help him prepare. Good luck!

The Chicagawan people have an established code of respect related to body language, gestures, and speech, including

- When sharing a meal together, allow your host to eat off of your plate whenever he or she chooses. You do not have the same option unless he or she offers explicitly.

The Chicagawa are a proud people who value respect from foreigners highly. Failure to show respect is a very serious insult, and they do not forgive easily. You are one of the cultural advisors to the new British ambassador to Chicagawa, a country that has just become important for Britain because of newly found oil reserves. You have been in Chicagawa only a short time, but you must help the ambassador prepare for his first reception with important Chicagawans. He is running late, and you and the other advisors have only 10 minutes to help him prepare. Good luck!

The Chicagawan people have an established code of respect related to body language, gestures, and speech, including

- When speaking to someone, the custom is to shake your left hand occasionally at the side of your head. This indicates that you are listening.

The Chicagawa are a proud people who value respect from foreigners highly. Failure to show respect is a very serious insult, and they do not forgive easily. You are one of the cultural advisors to the new British ambassador to Chicagawa, a country that has just become important for Britain because of newly found oil reserves. You have been in Chicagawa only a short time, but you must help the ambassador prepare for his first reception with important Chicagawans. He is running late, and you and the other advisors have only 10 minutes to help him prepare. Good luck!

The Chicagawan people have an established code of respect related to body language, gestures, and speech, including

- Showing the bottom of your feet or shoes is considered rude. This means that in crossing your legs or supporting your leg with the knee of the other is off limits.

The Chicagawa are a proud people who value respect from foreigners highly. Failure to show respect is a very serious insult, and they do not forgive easily. You are one of the cultural advisors to the new British ambassador to Chicagawa, a country that has just become important for Britain because of newly found oil reserves. You have been in Chicagawa only a short time, but you must help the ambassador prepare for his first reception with important Chicagawans. He is running late, and you and the other advisors have only 10 minutes to help him prepare. Good luck!

The Chicagawan people have an established code of respect related to body language, gestures, and speech, including

- Never touch your throat or face in public. It is rude.

The Chicagawa are a proud people who value respect from foreigners highly. Failure to show respect is a very serious insult, and they do not forgive easily. You are one of the cultural advisors to the new British ambassador to Chicagawa, a country that has just become important for Britain because of newly found oil reserves. You have been in Chicagawa only a short time, but you must help the ambassador prepare for his first reception with important Chicagawans. He is running late, and you and the other advisors have only 10 minutes to help him prepare. Good luck!

The Chicagawan people have an established code of respect related to body language, gestures, and speech. When speaking publicly,
- Your head must never be higher than the head of the tallest people to whom you are speaking. Even if they are sitting, you may not stand higher than their level. If you are taller than they are, you must hunch down.

The Chicagawa are a proud people who value respect from foreigners highly. Failure to show respect is a very serious insult, and they do not forgive easily. You are one of the cultural advisors to the new British ambassador to Chicagawa, a country that has just become important for Britain because of newly found oil reserves. You have been in Chicagawa only a short time, but you must help the ambassador prepare for his first reception with important Chicagawans. He is running late, and you and the other advisors have only 10 minutes to help him prepare. Good luck!

The Chicagawan people have an established code of respect related to body language, gestures, and speech, including

- The Chicagawa speak beautiful English. However, they have rules that are unique to them. The following words are forbidden in Chicagawa:

    1. So
    2. Talk
    3. Answer
    4. Wasn't
    5. Good
    6. And

Briefing Sheet for the Chicagawan Nationals

The Chicagawa are a proud people who value respect from foreigners highly. You view the failure to show respect as an egregious insult, and you do not forgive easily. However, if foreigners recognize their mistakes and immediately make an effort to adopt your social rules, you are very forgiving.

You know that many countries are interested in establishing better relations with Chicagawa because scientists have recently discovered large oil reserves in your tiny nation. A new British ambassador has arrived and has invited you to hear a welcoming speech and attend the reception to follow. The ambassador is due to speak in 10 minutes but he appears to be running late. This doesn't disturb you because the Chicagawa are not obsessive about punctuality.

As you know, the Chicagawan people have an established code of respect related to body languages, gestures, and speech. This code includes the following:

When greeting,

- Chicagawa stick out their tongues when they greet each other.
- To show respect, one of the pair extends his or her right pinky and connects it with the other person's index finger ONLY for two shakes. Usually the taller person extends the pinky.

When speaking,

- Women are the head of the household and are respected as such. As a sign of respect, you do not look at women when addressing them.
- When speaking to a man, remember to refer to him by his first or full name or by his wife's last name. Never refer to him by his last name. For example, if you are meeting Serebe Falusi and his wife, Tebere Hansa, refer to the man as Serebe, Serebe Falusi, or Mr. Hansa, but NEVER as Mr. Falusi.
- When speaking to someone, your custom is to shake your left hand occasionally at the side of your head. This indicates that you are listening.

When speaking publicly,

- Your head must never be higher than the head of the tallest people to whom you are speaking. Even if they are sitting, you may not stand higher than their level. If you are taller than they are, you must hunch down.
- When speaking to a large group of people and they are mixed men and women, you must turn your back to the audience to speak.

- The Chicagawa speak beautiful English. However, they are forbidden to use the following words:
  1. So
  2. Talk
  3. Answer
  4. Wasn't
  5. Good
  6. And

Showing the bottom of one's feet or the bottom of one's shoes is considered rude.

Touching one's throat or face in public is a sign that a person is single.

The Chicagawa are very obvious when they think they have been insulted, although they may not say so in words. Use body language, gestures, and other non-verbal language to let the ambassador know if he or she says or does anything that upsets you.

Briefing Sheet for the British Expatriates

You've lived in Chicagawa for many years. You found out about it from a friend of a friend, and after you came on a vacation, you never left. You love the Chicagawa, and because it took you many years to learn their customs, you are worried that your new ambassador may not fully understand how sensitive the Chicagawa can be about such matters. You came today to meet and hear the new ambassador and make sure he or she doesn't embarrass you too much!

You have several jobs in this exercise:

- Familiarize yourself with the Chicagawan customs listed below. The ambassador's advisors also have a list, but it may include some mistakes. (None of his advisors are really familiar with the Chicagawa because they only arrived last week.)

- Greet and talk with the Chicagawa people in the culturally appropriate manner.

- Help smooth the relations between the British staff and the Chicagawa whenever possible. If the British staff commits a cultural faux pas, you may correct them, but be warned—they may not accept your help.

- After the simulation, help your teacher lead a discussion about what you saw, who broke what social rules, and how people changed once they realized their conduct may have been offensive.

Chicagawa Customs

The Chicagawa are a proud people who value respect from foreigners highly. You view the failure to show respect as an egregious insult, and you do not forgive easily. However, if foreigners recognize their mistakes and immediately make an effort to adopt your social rules, you are very forgiving.

You know that many countries are interested in establishing better relations with Chicagawa because scientists have recently discovered large oil reserves in your tiny nation. A new British ambassador has arrived and has invited you to hear a welcoming speech and attend the reception to follow. The ambassador is due to speak in 10 minutes but he appears to be running late. This doesn't disturb you because the Chicagawa are not obsessive about punctuality.

As you know, the Chicagawan people have an established code of respect related to body languages, gestures, and speech. This code includes the following:

When greeting,

- Chicagawa stick out their tongues when they greet each other.

- To show respect, one of the pair extends his or her right pinky and connects it with the other person's index finger ONLY for two shakes. Usually the taller person extends the pinky.

When speaking,

- Women are the head of the household and are respected as such. As a sign of respect, you do not look at women when addressing them.

- When speaking to a man, remember to refer to him by his first or full name or by his wife's last name. Never refer to him by his last name. For example, if you are meeting Serebe Falusi and his wife, Tebere Hansa, refer to the man as Serebe, Serebe Falusi, or Mr. Hansa, but NEVER as Mr. Falusi.

- When speaking to someone, your custom is to shake your left hand occasionally at the side of your head. This indicates that you are listening.

When speaking publicly,

- Your head must never be higher than the head of the tallest people to whom you are speaking. Even if they are sitting, you may not stand higher than their level. If you are taller than they are, you must hunch down.

- When speaking to a large group of people and they are mix of men and women, you must turn your back to the audience to speak.

- The Chicagawa speak beautiful English. However, they are forbidden to use the following words:

    1. So
    2. Talk
    3. Answer
    4. Wasn't
    5. Good
    6. And

Showing the bottom of one's feet or the bottom of one's shoes is considered rude.

Touching one's throat or face in public is a sign that a person is single.

The Chicagawa are very obvious when they think they have been insulted, although they may not say so in words. Use body language, gestures, and other non-verbal language to let the ambassador know if he or she says or does anything that upsets you.

Briefing Sheet for the New British Ambassador

Congratulations! You are the newest ambassador to Chicagawa, a tiny country that has become very important to Britain because of recently discovered oil reserves. The prime minister appointed you to build political bridges with this very proud nation. You have been warned that the Chicagawan people are very sensitive about foreigners respecting their culture. You have a difficult job of making the Chicagawa feel comfortable with British diplomatic efforts and be generous with their oil.

Today you are hosting a reception for Chicagawan honored guests as well as members of the expatriate community You will give a five-minute speech and then mingle with the guests. You only arrived in Chicagawa today but you have a small staff of cultural advisors who can advise you about Chicagawan customs. However, they have been in the country only one week! A contingent of long-term British expatriates will attend the reception as well.

You have 10 minutes to meet with your staff and prepare your speech. You do not have to follow any advice they give. If during the speech or reception, you think you may have received bad advice and are offending the Chicagawans, you should try to remedy the situation.

One thing you do know is that the Chicagawans make it very obvious when they are displeased.

17. At the Improv

Description

Students improvise a variety of situations in which they must solve a problem, work with a team, and/or think and act quickly.

Time

45–60 minutes, depending on class size and number of improvisations chosen

Materials

Improvisation Scenarios resource sheet

watch or clock

Class layout and grouping of students

For the first part of the lesson, students work in pairs and then join another pair for the improvisations. For the second part of the lesson, students sit in their normal seats and are called to the front randomly for group improvisations.

Procedure

1. Explain that being able to think on your feet and respond and interact quickly and decisively is an important aspect of learning a language. Tell the students that in

today's lesson they will be working first in groups and then as a class to improvise various situations.

2. Give them an example using a willing, capable student to help you. (You may ask the student beforehand if he or she is willing to volunteer to take part in an improvisation, but do not describe the specific situation.) Ask for a volunteer to be the timekeeper.

3. Explain that the student is Mr/s. Ifeelsick and you are Dr. Youlookfinetome. Mr/s. Ifeelsick is seeing the doctor who knows he or she is a hypochondriac. Ask the timekeeper to start the time and let everyone know when five minutes are up. Start the exchange, and if the student is struggling, help him or her by asking a question that will move the improvisation along.

4. After the exchange, ask the student how it went, what was difficult, and what was easy. Make sure to ask if he or she enjoyed the improv. Then ask the class how they think it went, what seemed difficult, and if they have any questions about the procedure.

5. Pair the students and place each pair with another pair to make groups of four. If you have an uneven number, modify the improvisation situation to accommodate all players. Tell the teams to choose a number between 1 and 10; then call out a number. The team that is closest to the number improvises first.

6. Explain that you will call out an improvisation situation with two roles. The observing team decides who plays what role on the improvisation team. The observing team must also keep track of time and take notes to give feedback after the improvisation. When all teams are ready, announce the scenario and roles for Pairs Improv 1 and begin the exercise. Give the pairs five minutes to act out the improvisation.

7. After five minutes, call, "TIME!" Tell the observing team they have three minutes to give feedback to the improvisation team. Remind the observing team that the feedback should be constructive—they cannot simply say, "I didn't like it" or "I liked it." They must give solid examples and suggestions for how the improv could be improved.

8. After three minutes, tell the teams that they will now switch. The team that just completed the improvisation will now assign roles, observe, keep track of time, and provide feedback. When all teams are ready, announce the scenario and roles for Pairs Improv 2 and tell the observing teams to begin the exercise. Give the pairs five minutes for the improvisation and three minutes for the feedback. Remind the observers that all feedback must be constructive.

9. After the groups have finished, explain that the class will now engage in group improvisations. You will announce an improvisational situation and quickly point randomly to students who must come up to the front and improvise as a group. Groups will have between seven and ten minutes for their improvisations. Answer any questions and begin the exercise by announcing Group Improv #1. (After the group gathers, you may want to repeat the scenario and make sure everyone knows their role.) If the improvisation begins to drag, stop it, ask what the problem is, and restart the same situation as soon as possible to keep momentum.

10. Repeat the exercise with the Group Improv situations below. You can also develop your own situations or ask the students to create them.

Assessment

You can assess the students informally by observing each student's choices of words and phrases and how well they join in non-scripted conversation.

Improvisation Scenarios

Pairs Improv 1

Situation: A person dies and goes to the gates of heaven, where she is interviewed by St. Peter to find out whether she will get in.

Roles:

1. Dead Person
2. St. Peter

Pairs Improv 2

Situation: Student goes to Paris for holiday and calls her boyfriend to tell him about it. He is very curious about how she spends her time there.

Roles:

1. Girl (on phone)
2. Boyfriend (on phone)

Group Improv 1

Situation: A patient who was in an accident has amnesia. He/she is in the hospital surrounded by his/her parents, girlfriend/boyfriend, friends, relatives, and doctors.

Roles:

1. Patient
2. Mother
3. Father
4. Grandma
5. Girlfriend/Boyfriend
6. Best Friend
7. Dr. Jones
8. Dr. Clay
9. Friend from school
10. Uncle Joe

Group Improv 2

Situation: Four aliens come to Earth and want to learn some English. Four people find them. The earthlings must teach them some basic phrases and words in English and try to explain what they mean.

Roles:

1. Alien #1
2. Alien #2
3. Alien #3
4. Alien #4
5. Earthling #1
6. Earthling #2
7. Earthling #3
8. Earthling #4

Group Improv 3

Situation: Five diplomats from different countries have gone sightseeing in New York City. A tour guide shows them around, and a policeman helps them when they get lost.

Roles:

1. Nigerian Diplomat
2. Thai Diplomat
3. Mexican Diplomat
4. Slovenian Diplomat
5. Australian Diplomat
6. Tour Guide
7. Policeman

Group Improv 4

Situation: The teachers' lounge, where teachers and staff discuss their students

Roles:

1. Math Teacher
2. English Teacher
3. School Secretary
4. Science Teacher
5. History Teacher
6. Principal
7. Counselor
8. Janitor

Group Improv 5

Situation: The student lunchroom, where students discuss school and their teachers

Roles:

1. Student #1
2. Student #2
3. Student #3
4. Student #4
5. Student #5
6. Student #6
7. Student #7
8. Student #8
9. Janitor

18. Panel of Experts

Instructional objectives

Students will be able to:

- focus attention selectively

- use written sources of information to support their oral presentations

- paraphrase, summarize, elaborate, clarify, ask relevant questions, and make relevant comments in conversation, debate, and simulations

- participate effectively in face-to-face conversations on assorted subjects

- negotiate and initiate conversations by questioning, restating, soliciting information, and paraphrasing the communication of others

- request and provide clarification to their ideas and those of others

- persuade, argue, negotiate, evaluate, and justify in a variety of contexts

- distinguish fact and opinion, draw inferences, draw conclusions, and summarize from written material

- describe or read about an unfamiliar activity or topic

Description

On small panels, students pose as experts on a variety of things. After the students present mini-biographies of what makes them an expert, the audience is encouraged to ask the panel questions to "stump" them.

Time

90 minutes, followed by a 20-minute wrap-up the following day

Materials

Panel Assignments resource sheet (optional)

Expert Tracking Sheet (copy for each student)

Question and Response Tracking Sheet (copy for each student)

Points Distribution Guidelines for Panel of Experts

Class layout and grouping of students

Place four chairs at the front of the room on one side of a long table or move four desks together. The class faces the panel.

Procedure

Day 1

1. Discuss what constitutes evidence and review its importance in proving an argument. Tell the students that expert opinion is often accepted as evidence. Brainstorm ideas for what they think makes an expert.

2. Now tell the students that they will play the role of experts on a panel. You may use Panel Assignments or you may ask students to call out ideas for the subject and roles. Choose four students or ask for volunteers and assign them their roles. Write the name of each on an Expert Tracking Sheet. Then tell the panel members to create a fictitious résumé that will convince the audience that they are experts. They may work alone or as a group. They have five minutes to do this.

3. Ask each expert to choose an assistant from the audience to serve as his or her secretary. Distribute a copy of Question and Response Tracking Sheet to each. The secretaries are responsible for recording the questions asked of their expert as well as a synopsis of their expert's response.

4. Tell the students that you will also keep track of each question (using your Expert Tracking Sheets) and later ask the audience how believable the experts were in answering each question. Each secretary should be on hand to provide a synopsis of the answer that his or her expert gave.

5. Answer any questions the students may have. Once the experts have finished writing their résumés, assemble the panel. Give the members five minutes total to introduce themselves and present their credentials. The class then has seven minutes to ask questions. The panel members must answer all questions. If they do not know an answer, they must make one up.

6. Remind the audience that you are looking for intelligent questions and because of time constraints they may ask each expert no more than four questions. If there is a lull in the questioning, you may need to jumpstart the discussion with a question or two. As the discussion progresses, write down each question asked on the appropriate Expert Tracking Sheet. Make sure that the secretaries are also writing down the questions and responses.

7. After seven minutes, stop the discussion. Read each of the questions asked of each of the panel members. After each question, ask the secretary to provide a synopsis of the answer. Then ask the students to raise their hands if they believed the response that the expert gave. Record the results on the sheet.

8. Ask the secretaries to give their Question and Response Tracking Sheets to their expert. Thank the panel and repeat the exercise until all students have had the opportunity to be experts.

9. Tell the students that for the next class, their assignment is to research the answers to the questions posed to them and reference the source.

Day 2

1. The students should have their questions, responses, and source sheets ready. Explain that you will now assign points to each expert based on the audience's reaction from yester-

day and the research the experts conducted as homework. Distribute Points Distribution Guidelines.

2. Ask the students who were on the first panel to come to the front of the room. Have one of the students read aloud his first question and response and indicate whether or not the answer he gave the previous day was fact. If it was not, have him give the correct response. If the answer the expert gave the previous day is correct AND if the expert can now provide proof of this, give the expert ten points.

3. As the expert finishes each question, refer back to the data you gathered yesterday on the Expert Tracking Sheet to see whether the majority believed the response or not. Assign points based on the Points Distribution Guidelines and note them on the sheet.

4. Add up the points for each expert to determine an overall winner.

Student Products

*   Secretaries for each expert will produce a list of questions and a synopsis of the answers their experts give.

*   Students will research the answers to the questions they answered as an expert and cite appropriate sources.

Assessment

Classmates will assess students' spoken word, body language, gestures, and presentation by voting on their credibility as experts. You can assess their research on the questions asked.

Extensions and modifications

Panel members can discuss the topic, citing expert evidence they have researched.

Panel Assignments

Relationships Panel

Dr. Barry Goldman—A psychiatrist

Joan Waters—A relationship coach

Anna Love—Married for 13 years and mother of two

John Andrews—Married six times

European Union Panel

Alan O'Hare—Prime Minister of United Kingdom

Agafia Montey—Foreign Affairs Officer to Uzbekistan

Basir Muzzafara—Turkish Ambassador to the United Nations

Dovidas Ligthah—Foreign Affairs Officer to Lithuania

Christmas Traditions Panel

Joop Van Horn—Dutch shop owner

Gillian Massey—English storyteller

Bruno Weiss—German toy maker

Paul Rogers—Canadian dogsled racer

Dieting

Dr. Joe Carbs—Creator of popular fad diet

Rabbi Gould—Rabbi from California

Maureen Finn—Actress who recently lost 50 kilos (110 lbs.)

Mahteab Otonga—Gold medal winner for men's marathon in 1996 Olympics

Expert Tracking Sheet

Expert name: _____

Panel subject: _____

Question 1: _____
_____

_____Majority believed
_____Majority did not believe

Points: _____

Question 2: _____
_____

_____Majority believed
_____Majority did not believe

Points: _____

Question 3: _____
_____

_____Majority believed
_____Majority did not believe

Points: _____

Question 4: _____
_____

_____Majority believed
_____Majority did not believe

Points: _____

Total Points: _____

Question and Response Tracking Sheet

Expert: _____

Secretary: _____

Question 1: _____

Response:_____

_____

_____

_____

Actual Answer: _____

_____

_____

Source(s): _____

_____

_____

Question 2: _____

Response:_____

_____

_____

_____

Actual Answer: _____

_____

_____

Source(s): _____

_____

_____

Question 3: _____

Response: _____

_____

_____

_____

Actual Answer: _____

_____

_____

Source(s): _____

_____

_____

Question 4: _____

Response: _____

_____

_____

_____

Actual Answer: _____

_____

_____

Source(s): _____

_____

_____

Points Distribution Guidelines for Panel of Experts

If the audience felt that the "expert" was making up the answer and it turns out that the expert was correct	+ 1
If the audience felt that the expert was making up the answer and it turns out that the expert did make it up	-1
If the audience felt that the answer that the expert gave to a question was believable and it turned out that the answer was fabricated	+1
If the audience felt that the answer that the expert gave to a question was believable and it turns out that the expert was right	+1
If a question asked of the expert does not have a reference such as a personal opinion, but the audience believed them	+1

19. Write, Read, Action!

<table>
<tr><td>

Instructional objectives

Students will be able to:

- follow oral and written directions
- give oral and written directions
- request and provide clarification of their ideas and those of others
- elaborate and extend other people's ideas and words
- review and give feedback on the work of others
- take notes to record important information and direct one's own learning
- analyze common tasks and be able to write out detailed how-to instructions

</td></tr>
</table>

Description

Students work in pairs to write detailed instructions of how to do common activities that other students then act out as the instructions are read.

Time

2 class sessions of 45–60 minutes

Materials

How to Wash and Dry the Dishes resource sheet

Outline for How to Wash and Dry the Dishes resource sheet (copy for each student)

Outline for Instructional Material activity sheet (copy for each student)

Class layout and grouping of students

Students initially will work in pairs. In the second part of the lesson, they will work in groups of six.

Procedure

Day 1

1. Organize the students into groups of six and ask each group to form pairs, labeled A, B, and C. Tell the class that each pair will write detailed instructions on how to perform a common activity. After they have completed the instructions, one pair in their group

will read their instructions while another pair acts them out. The remaining pair will takes notes and critique the instructions so that the pair who wrote them can revise them. The next day they will have a chance to read their narration again and have the pair that initially critiqued their writing act out their narration, while the pair that initially acted now does a critique.

2. Share the following example using How to Wash and Dry the Dishes resource sheet. Ask two outgoing volunteers to come to the front of the room. Assign one of them to be the washer and the other the dryer. Read the narration as the volunteers act it out.

3. After you finish reading, ask the class how the two volunteers did. Were any parts of the instructions confusing? Analyze the description and the acting with the class.

4. Distribute Outline for How to Wash and Dry the Dishes and Outline for Instructional Material, and review. Explain that when writing their instructions, the students should first develop an outline listing all the steps necessary to complete the task. They can then elaborate on the outline in their instructions.

5. Assign one of the three activities to each pair in the group. The activities are

   a. How two people wash a car

   b. How two people put up and decorate a Christmas tree

   c. How two people wrap a large present

6. Allow the students 30–40 minutes to write their instructions. Walk around the room to ensure that pairs are on the right track.

7. Tell Pair A to read their instructions to their group, while Pair B acts them out and Pair C takes notes so that they can offer a critique. When they are finished, instruct Pair C to present their critique. Pair A should take notes so that they can revise their instructions.

8. Repeat the exercise until all three groups have presented their instructions.

9. After the final critique, call the class to order and tell the students that they will have time in the next class period to further refine their work.

Day 2

1. Assemble the class in their groups and review yesterday's activity. Tell the class that the pairs will have 25 minutes to revise their instructions. As the students work, walk around the room to provide guidance where necessary.

2. After 25 minutes, Pair A presents their instructions while Pair C acts them out and Pair B takes notes and presents the critique.

3. Repeat the exercise until all pairs have presented. Make sure that a pair does not critique the same presentation it critiqued yesterday.

4. After the final critique, call the class to order and collect the final instructions. You may choose to ask if any pairs would like to volunteer to showcase their reading or acting for the group.

Student Products

Detailed instructions that have been through the revision process

Assessment

You can assess students informally as you walk around the room during pair work and as the pairs read their instructions. You can formally assess the final instructions.

Extensions and modifications

1. Allow the students to create their own situations. You judge whether a situation is appropriate.

2. Have the students act out descriptive passages and have them identify particular words that help to bring a situation to life.

How to Wash and Dry the Dishes

Note that for the purposes of this narration, dish refers to any reusable item that you can use for eating, serving, or cooking. It can be a plate, cup, glass, pan, pot, or other utensil.

First determine who will wash and who will dry. The washer makes sure he starts with a clean sink and then blocks the drain using a stopper. Next, he fills the sink three-fourths full with warm water. He then adds dishwashing soap to make the water sudsy. The washer also needs to make sure that he has a washing cloth, brush, or sponge to wash the dishes. He must also decide how to rinse the soapy dishes. One method is to fill an adjacent sink with clean warm water and dip the soapy dishes in it. The other method is to simply run the hot water to rinse over the soapy dish.

The dryer makes sure that there is an area for the washer to place the cleaned dishes so that the extra water drains off. (This also makes the process more efficient because the washer does not have to wait to hand off each dish to the dryer.) This area can be a countertop covered with a clean towel, a dish drainer, or an adjacent sink. The dryer also makes sure that he has one or two clean dish towels. Once the sink and the drying area are ready, they can begin.

The washer scrapes any large particles of food off the dirty dishes into the garbage. Then he stacks the dirty plates, cups, saucers, and cookware into separate piles next to the sink. The washer starts the process with the most delicate dishes, such as glassware and cups, first and then moves on to plates and bowls. Finally, he washes the cookware. The washer may place stacks of dirty dishes into the soapy water to allow the items to soak, or he may wash each item separately. Whatever he decides, the washer should handle each dirty dish with care and use the sponge, cloth, or brush to wipe the surfaces of the dish until it is clean. The washer then rinses the dish in whichever manner he has chosen and places it in the drying area.

The dryer picks up the wet dish and uses a towel to dry all surfaces. He then either puts the dish in its proper place or, if he does not know where to put it, stacks it in a clean area of the kitchen for storage later. Once he has finished drying the dish, he repeats the process with the other wet dishes.

When the washer finishes all the dishes, he pulls the plug from the drain and empties the sink of dirty water. He then uses the cloth or sponge to wipe down any wet surfaces near the sink and wipe down the inside of the sink, taking care to remove food particles and other trash that may have collected near the drain.

When the sink area is clean and all the dishes have been properly washed and dried, the team has successfully washed and dried the dishes!

Outline for How to Wash and Dry the Dishes

Activity: How to Wash and Dry the Dishes

Roles involved in activity: Washer, Dryer

General activities associated with each role: Washer must clean and fill sink, get a sponge or cloth, scrape dishes, stack dishes, wash dishes, rinse dishes, and clean sink and adjacent area. Dryer must make a clean area for wet dishes, find and use clean towel, dry and store dishes.

Steps for each role:

1. Preparation

Washer

    a. Start with a clean sink

    b. Block drain

    c. Fill sink with warm water

    d. Add soap

    e. Get a washcloth, brush, or sponge

    f. Decide how to rinse the soapy dishes—dip soapy dishes into clean warm water or run hot water tap

Dryer

    a. Find clean place for wet dishes

    b. Find 1–2 towels

2. Activity

Washer

    a. Scrape dirty dishes

    b. Stack dirty items next to the sink or in water

    c. Carefully wash with sponge, cloth, or brush

d. Rinse dish

e. Place clean dish in drying area

Dryer

a. Dry dish

b. Put dish away or stack in a clean area

c. Continue drying another dish

3. Completion

Washer

a. When finished washing, drain sink

b. Wipe down any wet surfaces near the sink

c. Wipe down inside of the sink and remove food particles and trash in sink

Dryer

None

Extra Notes:

First you need to determine who will wash and who will dry.

Dish = any reusable item that you can use for eating, serving, or cooking. It can be a plate, cup, glass, pan, pot, or other utensil.

The washer should start to wash the most sensitive dishes, such as glassware and cups, first then move on to plates and bowls, and finally wash pots, pans, or skillets.

Activity Sheet
Outline for Instructional Material

When writing instructions you must describe each step in detail, to leave no room for errors or questions. The best way to make sure you do not forget a step is to use an outline such as that below. Then you can write your detailed instructions.

Activity: _____

Number and name of roles involved in activity: _____

_____

General activities associated with each role: _____

_____

Steps for each role:

1. Preparation

      Role 1:

      Role 2:

      Etc.

2. Activity:

      Role 1:

      Role 2:

      Etc.

3. Completion

      Role 1:

      Role 2:

      Etc.

Extra Notes: _____

_____

20. Session of the Security Council

Instructional objectives

Students will be able to: ·

- demonstrate good comprehension during a variety of exchanges by verbally responding appropriately
- respond critically to the opinions and views of others
- actively participate in full-class discussion
- work in team to achieve common goals
- use written sources of information to support their oral presentations
- use the appropriate degree of formality with different audiences and settings
- analyze the social context to determine appropriate language use
- practice variations for language in different social settings

Description

Students are involved in a role play of a session of the UN Security Council, focusing on resolving a fictitious conflict. They will research and present their nation's stand on the issue and then attempt to negotiate a possible solution.

Time

2 class sessions: 1 of 45 minutes and 1 of 60–90 minutes

Materials

Global Security Issues resource sheet (optional)

UN Security Council Country List resource sheet

Country Profile activity sheet (copy for each student)

Rules of Procedure for the UN Secretary General

names of Security Council countries on cardboard (to be placed in front of each student team)

timer

Preparation

1. Select an issue for the class to address during the session (see Global Security Issues for some suggestions).

2. Select the non-permanent members of the Security Council from the options on the UN Security Council Country List.

3. You will need to conduct the student preparation one to two weeks before the session.

Class layout and grouping of students

Set up the classroom to resemble the Security Council chamber, with the tables and chairs either forming a circle or a square, so that all student teams face each other.

Procedure

One to Two Weeks before the Lesson

1. Explain to the students that in a week or two they will participate in a simulation of a UN Security Council session. Explain that the Security Council is the arm of the United Nations that has the responsibility to maintain peace and security among nations. It has the power to make decisions that governments that are members of the United Nations must abide by. The Security Council is made up of fifteen member states, five of which are permanent members and ten of which are temporary seats. The permanent five are China, France, Russia, the United Kingdom, and the United States. For further information on the UN and its Security Council, check out www.un.org/sc/.

2. Divide the students into groups of two or three (depending on the size of the class) and assign a country to each group. You should have fifteen groups.

3. Announce the topic of the session. Use current events such as the crisis in Darfur, the conflict between Eritrea and Ethiopia, or maybe the Middle East crisis. You will need to be specific—a list of possible topics is given below.

4. Distribute the blank Country Profile sheets. Tell the delegations that they have one or two weeks to do the following:

   - Research their country and complete the country profile
   - Research the issue, and how their country stands on it

5. When the session convenes, each country will offer a three-minute speech clearly stating where it stands on the issue. Then they will meet with another delegation to develop a proposal to solve the problem.

6. Remind the groups to work together on the assignment and choose the delegates who will present their positions.

7. After all groups have prepared, choose a flexible, outgoing student to be the UN secretary general and provide him or her with a copy of the Rules of Procedure.

During the Session

1. Place the country nameplates on the desks and ask the delegations to take their seats behind the appropriate plate. Remind the delegations of how the meeting will proceed.

2. Invite the UN secretary general to conduct the meeting. As the meeting progresses, keep track of time and prompt the secretary general if he or she is confused about the next step in the process.

3. Once the session is complete, debrief the exercise. You may use the following questions:

- Were there any disagreements during the caucus sessions on how to address the crisis? How did you handle them?

- What lines of reasoning did your caucus present in support of your solution?

- Did the language you used in this diplomatic session differ from what you would use in another context?

- Why is the language of diplomacy important?

Assessment

You can informally assess students during the country presentations and during their interactions in the caucus session. You also will be able to evaluate how well they present new proposals with limited preparation time and how well they stepped into their roles.

Global Security Issues

1. Avian flu virus has mutated with a human flu virus. The first outbreak of deadly flu took place in one of the northern provinces of China. If the virus is not contained, it can spread worldwide and kill 20% of the affected population.

2. Iran has developed a nuclear weapon and has recently threatened to attack Israel. Israel has declared a state of national emergency and has promised to retaliate. The United States has responded by saying that in case of any attack on Israel it will use its nuclear arsenal against Iran.

3. The United States has decided to withdraw all its forces from Iraq. The situation in the country has deteriorated further, and violent clashes have erupted between the Sunnis and the Shiites. There is a real possibility of a civil war in the country.

4. The situation in Kashmir has worsened. Following violent clashes between Indian and Pakistani forces in the region and a number of civilian casualties on both sides, the two countries have come to a military standoff, and pro-war rhetoric is building. Both countries are in possession of nuclear weapons.

5. Zimbabwean dictator Robert Mugabe has ordered the white population to leave the country. About 80,000 people have been rounded up and some have been driven to the border areas with neighboring Botswana and Mozambique. Clashes with the police have resulted in civilian casualties. Botswana's government, working together with the UN High Commission for Refugees, has prepared for the outpour of refugees. The United Kingdom has warned the Zimbabwean government that it is considering military action to protect the refugees and stop evictions and forced displacement.

UN Security Council Country List

PERMANENT MEMBERS:

China, France, Russia, United Kingdom, United States

NON-PERMANENT MEMBERS:

Option 1:

Albania, Bosnia-Herzegovina, Canada, Ecuador, Hungary, Indonesia, Netherlands, Portugal, Romania, Zambia

Option 2:

Argentina, Bolivia, Cameroon, Denmark, Ethiopia, India, Kazakhstan, Lithuania, Thailand, Zambia

Options 3:

Australia, Botswana, Czech Republic, Malaysia, Moldova, Peru, Sweden, Turkey, Singapore, Ukraine

Option 4:

Angola, Austria, Bangladesh, Chile, Kenya, New Zealand, Pakistan, Uruguay, Tanzania, Venezuela

Option 5:

Algeria, Cambodia, Croatia, Egypt, Haiti, Macedonia, Mexico, Poland, Uganda, Zimbabwe.

Country Profile

Country Name: _____

Capital: _____

Official language(s):_____

_____

Population:_____

Neighbors:_____

_____

Political system:_____

Economic profile:_____

Recent history (up to 200 words):_____

_____

_____

_____

_____

_____

_____

_____

_____

_____

_____

_____

Stand on the topic being discussed in Security Council:_____

_____

_____

_____

_____

Alliances:_____

_____

_____

Disputes:_____

_____

_____

Rules of Procedure for the UN Secretary General

1. Welcome all the representatives and introduce the issue for consideration (up to five minutes).

2. Ask the country delegations to present their stand on the issue. Each presentation should not be longer than three minutes. You may want to inform the presenters that you will give them two signals: at one minute and at thirty seconds before their time elapses.

3. After the last presentation, call for a break and invite the country representatives to caucus another delegation to develop a joint proposal on the issue. Move from one group to another and assist the delegations with negotiations. Caucuses should be allowed to last no more than twenty minutes.

4. Invite the caucuses to present their solutions. Allow each group up to five minutes for its presentation.

5. Conclude the proceedings by thanking all the country representatives for participating in the session.

Chapter 5
Student Evaluation

Determining whether your students have mastered the learning objectives of a lesson requires evaluation. This can take many forms, but most teachers unfortunately restrict their evaluations to written exams or tests.

Deliberative methodology is a hands-on teaching technique that is generally incompatible with these traditional forms of assessment. It requires teachers to use rubrics to evaluate the students as they debate, give a speech, role-play, etc. This section explains why using rubrics is important and discusses how to develop and use them.

What is a rubric?

A rubric is a tool used to score a student's progress or skill. It consists of an even number of point values listed across the top of a matrix and a list of skills and/or content sets along the side. These skills and/or content sets vary according to the work being evaluated and the educator's specific objectives. The rubric lists criteria for each skill along the point value scale, with high skill exhibition correlated to the highest point value and progressively lower skill exhibition assigned to progressively lower point values.

Why use a rubric?

Rubrics are very helpful in assessing learning in a way that is measurable and meaningful to students. They make teacher expectations very clear and help students keep track of their performance and measure progress over time.

Rubrics permit peer evaluation that is understandable and constructive. Often when students evaluate each other, they are unsure how to provide feedback. Rubrics allow students to give very specific feedback with no training and are an easy tool for students to understand and administer.

Rubrics typically reduce the amount of time teachers spend evaluating student work. You will find that in using a rubric, all aspects of the work have been addressed, with no need to provide extensive written comments to explain a grade. If you want to stress an aspect of a student's work, you can simply circle the criteria or skill in the rubric, rather than struggle to explain the flaw or strength you have noticed.

Best of all, rubrics accommodate a wide variety of learning abilities and styles. You can create rubrics for students with special needs or develop separate criteria that are specific to their learning plan. While the three rubrics presented here have four gradations of quality for each criterion, you can modify them to suit the specific needs of your students.

How do I use one?

Take a look at the rubric for speech and presentations below: The rubric lists the skill criteria in the column on the left. The skills being evaluated include body language, eye contact, introduction and closure, pacing, poise, voice, and content. The four columns to the right of the criteria describe varying degrees of quality, from excellent to poor, with each assigned a point value. As concisely as possible, these columns explain what makes a good presentation or speech good and a bad one bad.

The criteria in a rubric must meet the learning objectives for the lesson. This means that if a student is giving a speech on types of world government and your objective is for students to be able to describe at least four main types, your rubric criteria should focus on knowledge presented, detail given, etc. It should NOT focus on aspects of good speech. If, on the other hand, the lesson has two objectives—knowing government types and describing them clearly to a group, part of the rubric should focus on content and part on presentation.

To use a rubric that you developed for a deliberative methodology activity, distribute it in advance of the presentation, debate, or role play and explain it to your students. When it is time for a student to present, fill out the student information such as name, work being evaluated, etc. on a new rubric form. As they present, fill out a form for each student. If there is a specific point you wish to emphasize, circle it or write a brief comment on the form. When the student has finished, tally the points and give a grade, such as 20 points out of a possible 24 or 20/24.

How do I teach my students to use a rubric to assess their peers?

Rubrics are great tools for students to easily and more precisely assess each other's work. While the teacher's assessment on a rubric should always be the data used to actually assign a grade or measurement, reviewing rubrics that students complete on their peers provides valuable feedback to the student and to the teacher to assess how well the rest of the class understood the work presented. For example, imagine that Student A gives a presentation on the elements of a story and Student B completes a rubric on Student A's performance. As Student B completes the rubric, he gives Student A low scores on every aspect but you give top scores on every aspect. This evaluation gives you valuable data on Student B—she does not fully understand the content or possibly she does not understand how to complete a rubric. Both pieces of data are important to know so that you can determine what content to reteach.

While the prospect of completing a rubric may seem intimidating at first, you can teach your students the basics with a simple 10-minute lesson. Keeping in mind that rubrics are to be tailored to the learning objectives of the lesson, use the following guide to teach the correct use of completing and reading a rubric.

How do I create a rubric?

We have presented three rubrics below, but you should learn how to create your own rubrics to tailor them to your teaching objectives. Math lessons, speeches, science experiments, debating, practicing a job interview—all can be evaluated with a rubric, provided its criteria meet the objectives. Here are the steps you need to create your rubrics:

1. Define the learning objectives you wish to measure. Typically these are the objectives for the lesson. You can finely tune this list as you develop your rubric.

2. Create a list of criteria to evaluate. Decide what counts in quality work. Avoid general, unhelpful descriptions like the "volume was bad." This tells us little about what the problem was—was it too soft, too loud? Rather, define lower levels of quality in a way that is simply descriptive of the work presented, such as, "the volume was too low for audience to hear speaker."

3. Articulate gradations of quality. Determine how many levels you want to create. Describe the best and worst levels of quality, and then fill in the middle levels. The more levels you create, the more defined the quality for each characteristic.

4. Distribute the rubric. Always distribute a blank copy of the rubric before you use it. This allows students to see exactly what defines excellence. It also defines the lesson's objectives clearly.

5. Use the rubric. For most deliberative methodology lessons, do not wait to complete a student's rubric—recall will not be sufficient to complete the rubric accurately. Fill out the rubric during the student presentation, before another presentation or activity begins. You can evaluate written work any time you have it available.

6. Return the completed rubric to the student immediately after you have recorded the points he has earned. This ensures that the work is still fresh in his mind.

7. Always give students time to revise their work based on the feedback they get in Step 6. This could mean rewriting an assignment or using the same rubric to evaluate another presentation on a different topic.

8. When students evaluate each other, use the same rubric that you use to evaluate student work. Consistency of evaluation instruments is key to reliable and valid evaluation information.

Three Deliberative Methodology Rubrics

Review the three deliberative methodology rubrics provided below. Note that these rubrics are tied to learning objectives about aspects of giving a speech or presentation, participating in a debate, and taking part in a role play or simulation. Feel free to use them as they are or to start creating your own. See the Resources section at the end of the book for other rubric resources.

Debate Rubric

Student/Team Name: _____

Side: _____

Topic: _____

	4	3	2	1	Points Earned
Eye Contact	Holds attention of entire audience with the use of direct and appropriate eye contact	Fairly consistent use of direct eye contact with most of the audience	Displays minimal eye contact with all of the audience. OR Focuses on only 1 or 2 people	No eye contact with audience	
Opening Statement	Team accurately and clearly outlines content of team's speeches; captures the attention of the audience	Team delivers opening statement clearly; statement is organized	Team does not outline content of speeches; some disorganization	Team's opening statements are confusing or non-existent	
Closure	Student delivers opening and closing remarks that capture the attention of the audience and set the mood	Introductory and closing remarks are clearly delivered	Student clearly uses either an introductory or closing remark, but not both	Student does not display clear introductory or closing remarks	
Pacing	Student meets time interval nearly exactly	Delivery is well-paced, but does not meet apportioned time interval	Delivery is given in bursts and does not meet apportioned time interval	Delivery is either too quick or too slow to meet apportioned time interval	
Poise	Student appears relaxed and self-confident, makes no mistakes in articulation or body language	Makes minor mistakes but quickly recovers from them; displays little tension	Displays mild tension; has trouble recovering from mistakes	Tension and nervousness are obvious; has trouble recovering from mistakes	

	4	3	2	1	Points Earned
Voice	Use of fluid speech and inflection maintains the interest of the audience; consistent appropriate volume	Satisfactory use of inflection, inconsistent use of fluid speech; mostly maintains consistency of appropriate volume	Displays some level of voice inflection throughout delivery; volume sometimes inappropriate	Consistently speaks in a monotone voice; volume consistently inappropriate	
Argument	Evidence is well-researched and presented; all points are addressed; arguments are clear and well understood	Evidence is present; most major points are addressed; arguments are mostly clear	Evidence is not consistently given; 2 or more major points are not addressed; arguments are confusing to follow	Topic and/or all major points are not addressed; no evidence is presented; arguments make no/little sense	
Rebuttal	Refuting opposition is respectful yet to the point; rebuttal always supported by evidence; all points raised by opposition are sufficiently addressed	Refuting opposition is mostly respectful yet to the point; rebuttal mostly supported by evidence; most points raised by opposition are sufficiently addressed	Refuting opposition is sometimes disrespectful; rebuttal lacks some clarity and/or evidence; some points raised by opposition are insufficiently addressed	Disrespect is shown to opposing team; rebuttal is confusing or does not respond to points raised	

Total Points _____

Score: _____ / 32

Speeches and Presentations Rubric

Student / Group Name: _____

Speech / Presentation Title: _____

	4	3	2	1	Points Earned
Body Language	Movements are fluid and help the audience visualize	Movements and/or gestures are neutral in affecting presentation	Very little movement or descriptive gestures OR Movement or gestures are somewhat distracting	No movement or descriptive gestures OR Movement and/or descriptive gestures are distracting and take away from presentation	
Eye Contact	Holds attention of entire audience with the use of direct and appropriate eye contact	Fairly consistent use of direct eye contact with most of the audience	Displays minimal eye contact with all of the audience. OR Focuses on only 1-2 people	No eye contact with audience	
Introduction and Closure	Student delivers open and closing remarks that capture the attention of the audience and set the mood	Introductory and closing remarks are clearly delivered	Student clearly uses either an introductory or closing remark but not both	Student does not display clear introductory or closing remarks	
Pacing	Student meets time interval nearly exactly	Delivery is well-paced but does not meet apportioned time interval	Delivery is given in bursts and does not meet apportioned time interval	Delivery is either too quick or too slow to meet apportioned time interval	

	4	3	2	1	Points Earned
Poise	Student appears relaxed and self-confident, makes no mistakes in articulation or body language	Makes minor mistakes but quickly recovers from them; displays little tension	Displays mild tension; has trouble recovering from mistakes	Tension and nervousness are obvious; has trouble recovering from mistakes	
Voice	Use of fluid speech and inflection maintains the interest of the audience	Satisfactory use of inflection, inconsistent use of fluid speech	Displays some level of voice inflection throughout delivery	Consistently speaks in a monotone voice	
Content	Content is well thought out; arguments are clear and well understood	Content is organized; there is some confusion in speech	Content is not well-organized but major topics are addressed	Content is disorganized; does not address the topic at hand	

Total Points _____

Score: _____ / 28

Role Play / Simulations Rubric

Student / Group Name:_____

Situation: _____

Role:_____

	4	3	2	1	Points Earned
Planning	Interprets the situation creatively and without prompting; plans dialogue and action that deepens the characterization or reinforces the dramatic situation	Interprets the situation imaginatively and with little prompting; plans dialogue and action that is appropriate to the characters and situation	Interprets the situation literally and with some prompting; plans dialogue and action that is conventional but is mostly appropriate to the characters and dramatic situation	Interprets the situation with difficulty and much prompting; plans dialogue and action that is superficial, stereotypical, or inappropriate to the characters and dramatic situation	
Preparing	Shows leadership while planning and rehearsing	Makes constructive contributions while planning and rehearsing	Makes some constructive contributions while planning and rehearsing	Makes very few constructive contributions while planning and rehearsing	
Speaking in Role	Speaks very audibly, clearly, and expressively in their assigned role	Speaks audibly, clearly, and somewhat expressively in their assigned role	Speaks audibly and clearly in their assigned role	Speaks inaudibly, unclearly, and inconsistently in their assigned role	
Action	Uses movement and body language in a consistently expressive, appropriate, and creative way	Uses movement and body language often in an expressive and appropriate way	Uses some movement and body language expressively and appropriately	Uses little or no movement and/or body language expressively and appropriately	

	4	3	2	1	Points Earned
Reflecting and Understanding	Reaches the overall goal of the activity; is able to make generalizations about the characters and dramatic situation	Mostly reaches the overall goal of the activity; can make inferences about the characters and dramatic situation	Partially reaches the overall goal of the activity; somewhat confused about how characters and situations relate to the subject	Does not have an understanding of the overall goal; very confused about the relation of the situation and the lesson being taught	
Teamwork	Respectful of others on team; encourages others' contributions	Works largely with team, as a team; values others' contributions	Sometimes it is not apparent that student is part of a team; indifferent to others	Disrespectful of others or of their assigned roles; doesn't work with team at all	

Total Points _____

Score: _____/ 24

Glossary

Affirmative

The side or team in a debate that supports the resolution.

Argument

A controversial statement, frequently called a claim, supported by grounds (evidence) and a warrant. The standards of a logically good argument include acceptability, relevance, and sufficiency.

Argument Construction

The process of formulating a debate or exchange that is for or against some particular viewpoint.

Articulation

To pronounce or say words clearly and slowly.

Assessment

A formative, process-oriented, reflective, diagnostic means of deciding how well material has been understood and retained.

Ballot

A sheet of paper on which the judge records the decision (who won the debate), the reasons for the decision (why that team won), and speaker points awarded to each debater.

Brainstorming

A process of listing as many ideas that an individual or group can think of on a topic.

Categorize

Organize material into meaningful groups or classes.

Claim

A controversial statement an arguer supports using reason. Claims can be fact claims, policy claims, or value claims.

Coaching

A pedagogical methodology in which the teacher gently guides a class discussion, largely allowing the students to run it. As a coach, the teacher does not give direct instruction nor even provide answers to questions raised. The coach directs questions back to the students to ponder and answer.

Code-Word System

A language acquisition technique whereby learners link words in their native tongue with new target language vocabulary using mental visual representations.

Communication Skills

Speaking and listening are the communication skills most critical to successful language acquisition.

Con

The two person negative team in Public Forum debate.

Constructive Criticism

To make positive comments about a performance so as to motivate and educate.

Constructive Speech

A speech that presents a debater's basic arguments for or against the resolution.

Cooperative Learning

A learning technique in which students are placed in small teams, typically comprised of students with different levels of ability, and are expected to work together to achieve an end goal.

Credibility

The quality of being thought believable or trustworthy.

Criteria

In debate, that which must be proven to win; the most important values or standards.

Critical Listener

A person who listens carefully, evaluates what they hear, and remembers important information.

Critical Thinking

The mental process in which one conceptualizes, analyzes, and evaluates information to reach a conclusion.

Critique

An oral evaluation of a presentation.

Cross-Examination

A period during a debate when a member of one team asks questions of a member of the opposing team.

Debate

The process of arguing about claims in situations where a judge must decide the outcome.

Debate Format

The arrangement of a debate with rules establishing time limits, speaking order, and the manner in which a debate will be conducted.

Decision

The judge's determination of which side won a debate.

Deliberative Methodology

A set of teaching approaches that utilize debate, role plays, simulations, speeches, and presentations to build critical thinking skills in a variety of subjects.

Direct Quotation

To read evidence word for word to support a claim.

ESL/EFL

English as a Second Language/English as a Foreign Language.

Evaluation

A summative, product-oriented, prescriptive tool that judges whether a student has retained the material taught.

Evidence

Different types of information (facts, statistics, theories, opinions, or narratives) that are used to support arguments. Evidence can be divided into two categories: that relating to reality (facts, theories, and presumptions) and that relating to preference (values, value hierarchies, and value categories).

Flow Sheet

Notes taken during a debate, usually written in columns, that enable the user to trace the progression of arguments.

Framework

A time line of expected skills and content to be taught and learned in a particular subject.

Government Team

The team affirming the resolution in a parliamentary debate. Also called the gov.

Impromptu Speaking

Speaking with little to no preparation time.

Interactive Instruction

Instruction that relies on student-teacher discussion, communication, and/or collaboration to reach a learning objective.

Instructional Objectives

A statement that describes the outcome of a specific educational activity, usually tied to the standards within the curricular framework.

Leader of the Opposition

The first oppositional speaker in parliamentary debate.

Loci Method

A technique whereby the learner imagines walking through the rooms of a familiar building, all the while connecting a part of the information to be learned with each room.

Member of the Government

The affirmative speaker who speaks after the Leader of the Opposition in parliamentary debate.

Member of the Opposition

The negative speaker who speaks after the Member of the Government in parliamentary debate.

Methodology

Principles or procedures for a discipline. In this text, it refers to educational techniques or approaches.

Mnemonics

A formula or rhyme that a learner uses to remember something.

Monotone

An unvarying tone of voice.

Narrative

A story or account of events.

Negative

The side in a debate that rejects the resolution.

Opponent

In debate, the term used to describe the other team.

Opposition

The team negating the propositional team in parliamentary debate. The opposition opposes the proposition.

Parliamentary Debate (National Parliamentary Debate Association)

A debate format in which the two teams take on the role of governmental leaders. This format requires a different topic for every round.

Parliamentary Debate (World's Style or European/British Parliament)

A version of parliamentary debate in which four teams compete at the same time, two for the proposition and two for the opposition.

Plan

When debating a proposition of policy, the course of action the affirmative proposes to solve the problems identified in the "need."

Policy Debate

A debate format that focuses on a current (usually a governmental) policy. Typically debaters have the same topic for the entire school year and read evidence, word for word.

Preparation Time

The time allotted to each team for preparation during a debate (eight minutes in Karl Popper debate).

Prime Minister

The first propositional speaker in a parliamentary debate.

Pro

The two-person affirmative team in a public forum debate.

Propositional

The team opposing the oppositional team in parliamentary debate. The propositional team supports the proposition.

Public Forum

An audience-oriented debate forum that does not usually allow expert debate judges. Topics are new each month and are chosen for their balance of evaluative arguments on both sides.

Rebuttal Speeches

The speeches in the debate that challenge and defend arguments introduced in the constructive speeches.

Refutation

The process of attacking and defending arguments.

Research

The process of locating and selecting evidence in preparation for a presentation.

Roadmap

A statement given at the beginning of a speech that lets the audience know the order of the speech.

Role Play

An exercise in which the participants assume the identity of a character in a scenario.

Scope and Sequence

A charted curricular plan in which a range of instructional objectives, skills, and content is organized.

Simulation

An exercise in which participants are given extensive documentation and background to take on a role in a scenario. Participants are usually asked to make difficult decisions.

Socratic Discussion

A teaching methodology in which the teacher or student(s) pose questions to the group in an attempt to reach some kind of truth or understanding. Rarely is there only one right answer, or sometimes even any answer at all.

Standards

Broadly stated expectations of what students should know and be able to do in particular subjects.

Statistics

Evidence expressed in numbers.

Status Quo

The current course of action; the present system.

Story Building

A technique in which the learner invents a story using the new vocabulary to be learned.

Strand

Curricular theme or topic.

Style

The use of language, voice, and body language in a presentation.

Theory

A statement that explains other facts or that predicts the occurrence of events.

Thesis Statement

A one-sentence statement given at the beginning of a debate or speech that lets the audience know the purpose: to inform, to persuade, or to entertain.

Warrant

In a debate, a stated or unstated reasoning process that explains the relationship between the evidence and the claim.

Resources

If you want to find out more about deliberative methodology for EFL and other subjects, check out the following Web sites:

Deliberative Methodology Information

Debatabase—a database of debate topics

http://www.idebate.org/debatabase/index.php

Debating Links

http://www.idebate.org/resources/links.php

International Debate Education Association homepage

www.idebate.org

National Forensic League

http://www.nflonline.org/Main/HomePage

English as a Foreign Language

Center for Applied Linguistics

http://www.cal.org

National Clearinghouse for English Language Acquisition and Language Instruction Educational Programs

http://www.ncela.gwu.edu/resabout/

Evaluation

Alternative Assessment Toolbox

http://jonathan.mueller.faculty.noctrl.edu/toolbox/rubrics.htm

Chicago Public Schools Rubric Bank

http://intranet.cps.k12.il.us/Assessments/Ideas_and_Rubrics/Rubric_Bank/rubric_bank.html